BEATING THE COMFORT TRAP

WINDY DRYDEN was born in London in 1950. He has worked in psychotherapy and counselling for over twenty years and is the author or editor of over ninety books, including *The Incredible Sulk* (Sheldon Press, 1992) and *Ten Steps to Positive Living* (Sheldon Press, 1994). Dr Dryden is Professor of Counselling at Goldsmiths' College, University of London.

Born in Dundee, Scotland, JACK GORDON is a graduate member of the British Psychological Society. He trained in Rational-Emotional Therapy under Professor Dryden and devotes his time to counselling and writing on RET.

Windy Dryden and Jack Gordon are also the authors of *Think Your Way to Happiness* and *How to Untangle Your Emotional Knots* (Sheldon 1990 and 1991).

Overcoming Common Problems Series

For a full list of titles please contact
Sheldon Press, Marylebone Road, London NW1 4DU

Overcoming Common Problems Series

Curing Arthritis Diet Book
MARGARET HILLS

Curing Arthritis – The Drug-Free Way
MARGARET HILLS

Curing Arthritis
More ways to a drug-free life
MARGARET HILLS

Curing Illness – The Drug-Free Way
MARGARET HILLS

Depression
DR PAUL HAUCK

Divorce and Separation
Every woman's guide to a new life
ANGELA WILLANS

Everything Parents Should Know About Drugs
SARAH LAWSON

Gambling – A Family Affair
ANGELA WILLANS

Good Stress Guide, The
MARY HARTLEY

Heart Attacks – Prevent and Survive
DR TOM SMITH

Helping Children Cope with Bullying
SARAH LAWSON

Helping Children Cope with Divorce
ROSEMARY WELLS

Helping Children Cope with Grief
ROSEMARY WELLS

Helping Children Cope with Stammering
DR TRUDIE STEWART AND JACKIE TURNBULL

Hold Your Head Up High
DR PAUL HAUCK

How to Be Your Own Best Friend
DR PAUL HAUCK

How to Cope when the Going Gets Tough
DR WINDY DRYDEN AND JACK GORDON

How to Cope with Bulimia
DR JOAN GOMEZ

How to Cope with Difficult Parents
DR WINDY DRYDEN AND JACK GORDON

How to Cope with Difficult People
ALAN HOUEL WITH CHRISTIAN GODEFROY

How to Cope with Splitting Up
VERA PEIFFER

How to Cope with Stress
DR PETER TYRER

How to Enjoy Your Retirement
VICKY MAUD

How to Improve Your Confidence
DR KENNETH HAMBLY

How to Interview and Be Interviewed
MICHELE BROWN AND GYLES BRANDRETH

How to Keep Your Cholesterol in Check
DR ROBERT POVEY

How to Love and Be Loved
DR PAUL HAUCK

How to Pass Your Driving Test
DONALD RIDLAND

How to Stand up for Yourself
DR PAUL HAUCK

How to Start a Conversation and Make Friends
DON GABOR

How to Stick to a Diet
DEBORAH STEINBERG AND DR WINDY DRYDEN

How to Stop Smoking
GEORGE TARGET

How to Stop Worrying
DR FRANK TALLIS

How to Survive Your Teenagers
SHEILA DAINOW

How to Untangle Your Emotional Knots
DR WINDY DRYDEN AND JACK GORDON

How to Write a Successful CV
JOANNA GUTMANN

Hysterectomy
SUZIE HAYMAN

The Incredible Sulk
DR WINDY DRYDEN

The Irritable Bowel Diet Book
ROSEMARY NICOL

The Irritable Bowel Stress Book
ROSEMARY NICOL

Is HRT Right for You?
DR ANNE MacGREGOR

Jealousy
DR PAUL HAUCK

Learning to Live with Multiple Sclerosis
DR ROBERT POVEY, ROBIN DOWIE AND GILLIAN PRETT

Living with Angina
DR TOM SMITH

Overcoming Common Problems Series

Overcoming Common Problems

BEATING
THE COMFORT TRAP

Dr Windy Dryden and
Jack Gordon

sheldon PRESS

First published in Great Britain 1993
Sheldon Press, SPCK, Marylebone Road, London NW1 4DU

Third impression 1997

British Library Cataloguing in Publication Data

A catalogue record for this book is available from the British Library

ISBN 0–85969–660–X

Photoset by Deltatype Ltd, Ellesmere Port, Cheshire
Printed and bound in Great Britain by
Biddles Ltd, Guildford and King's Lynn

Contents

Introduction

What is the 'Comfort Trap'?

Some people may look at the title of this book and exclaim: 'What does it mean, the "Comfort Trap"? Do you mean' they might go on, 'that feeling comfortable is some kind of trap? What are you authors, a couple of hairshirt enthusiasts?' Our response would be a very definite 'Quite the contrary!' And our credentials speak for themselves: no one who knows us well would believe for one moment that we would even remotely associate ourselves with the 'scourge-the-flesh' brigade. As our previous books will confirm, we believe it is good to feel healthily comfortable; we strongly believe in giving and receiving pleasure and in striving for individual personal happiness in this life for ourselves and for those we love, both in the short and long term. We not only believe in that philosophy, we also practise it. So, why the title *Beating the Comfort Trap*? Our aim in writing this book is twofold. First, to explain what we mean by the Comfort Trap and why it is likely to diminish, rather than enhance, the overall level of pleasure and satisfaction we gain from life; also to show exactly how people fall into the Comfort Trap; and to outline precisely what action must be taken in order to escape from the Comfort Trap. Second, we want to show you how to stay out of the Comfort Trap once you have broken free of it; and to invite you to consider the advantages of acquiring a truly comprehensive rational philosophy of life designed to help you to live a maximally creative and happy life.

Let us consider these aims in more detail.

Unfortunately, it is the case that many of the individuals we encounter in both our professional and private lives, and who we consider to be potentially capable of leading happy existences, achieve instead only a very limited level of satisfaction in their lives – or even none at all. These are intelligent, well-meaning people who *could* achieve their goals of living happily and relating well to others, but who, instead are frequently miserable and alone, and constantly at loggerheads with the very people they would like to get on well with.

'Why does this happen?' we ask ourselves. The answer is this: Comfort is fine – up to a point. But it is a fact of life that no one is spared from trouble, pain or inconvenience. *It cannot be avoided.* Now, if we wisely accepted that fact, we would uncomplainingly put up with the discomfort

1

caused by various unpleasant experiences and do what we could to change obnoxious circumstances so as to minimize or eliminate the pain or discomfort. No one likes performing unpleasant tasks or enjoys having his or her wishes frustrated, and there is no reason why we should like what we definitely don't like. But neither is there any reason why unpleasant or painful things should *not* happen to us. Such things exist; if they happen to us, they happen!

Unfortunately, many people refuse to accept the observation that they cannot realistically expect to be comfortable, or, at least, free of discomfort, *all* the time. Rather, what these people are insisting is that life shouldn't be uncomfortable and that they can't bear to be uncomfortable; some will even exclaim as much, indicating their low tolerance of frustration or discomfort. As a result of stoutly clinging to the belief that they have to be comfortable *at all times*, and that it is *unbearable* if they are not comfortable, people avoid facing up to the uncomfortable events and circumstances in their lives. Although potentially capable of tackling the basic problem confronting them which is causing their discomfort, such people fail to try to do anything constructive to change the unpleasant circumstances in their lives because of their refusal to tolerate *any* degree of temporary discomfort – even when they realize that it would be in their best long-term interests to do so. By taking the 'easy' way out of their difficulties, these people only succeed in prolonging their discomfort beyond what would have been really necessary for them to bear had they resolved their difficulties in the first place. In other words, they are in the Comfort Trap. *That is what the Comfort Trap means: refusing to tolerate frustration because it is uncomfortable; going for the pleasures of the moment or instant gratification without due regard for the longer term consequences, such as losing much more pleasure or comfort in the future; or refusing to tolerate a moderate but necessary degree of pain or discomfort in the present in order to benefit from avoiding a greater degree of pain or discomfort later.*

Granted that being in the Comfort Trap is ultimately self-defeating and likely to reduce, rather than enhance, your pleasure and satisfaction in living the one life you definitely know you have, it makes logical sense for us to show you exactly how you get into the Comfort Trap and what you can do to get out of it. These are, you will recall, the second and third parts of our primary aim, and they constitute the main themes and focus of the chapters which follow.

Our second aim is to show you how to stay out of the Comfort Trap altogether. In order to accomplish this, we will tell you what you probably need to know – the particular values or rational attitudes you would be wise to acquire if you want to get along well with yourself, other people, and in your business and private life.

In pursuit of this objective, and assuming too, that your main purpose in life is to live longer and more pleasureably as a healthy, fully functioning human being, what then are these values or rational attitudes which we suggest you would be well advised to acquire to aid and abet your potential for living a full and happy life? In the six chapters that make up this book, we show you how to acquire the components of a rational philosophy of life and we focus on certain commonplace themes. Of particular importance are the following values or attitudes which are the cornerstones of a rational philosophy of living.

High frustration tolerance Healthy individuals tolerate, without necessarily liking, the vicissitudes of life, and tend to go along with Reinhold Niebuhr by striving to ameliorate or change what they can change, accept what they cannot change, and have the wisdom to know the difference between the two. They also give themselves and others the right to be wrong and to refrain from damning themselves or others, as persons, even when they intensely dislike their own or others' unacceptable behaviour. They accept that all humans are fallible, and do not unrealistically expect them to be perfect. High frustration tolerance and self-discipline are demonstrated by showing that one does not have to get what one wants immediately and that one can unrebelliously buckle down to doing necessary but boring or uncomfortable tasks when it is in one's best interests to do so.

Self-acceptance Self-acceptance means that we accept ourselves as being valuable to ourselves because we are alive and have some capacity to enjoy ourselves. A key aspect of self-acceptance is that you refuse to measure your intrinsic worth, or worth to yourself, by your achievements, your popularity, your service to others, your devotion to a church or political cause or by what other people think of you. You simply choose to accept yourself unconditionally and completely avoid rating yourself, your person, in any way whatsoever. You achieve for the joy of achieving, or to better the quality of your existence rather than to prove something about you.

Acceptance of uncertainty As emotionally mature individuals, we accept that we live in a world of probability and chance, where absolute certainties do not exist, and perhaps never will. Although you may prefer a fair degree of order, you do not demand to know exactly what the future will bring or what will happen to you personally. You realize that it can be quite fascinating and exciting to live in a probabilistic world where nothing is absolutely guaranteed, and it definitely is not horrible or unbearable.

Risk-taking Realizing that all life involves risk, emotionally healthy men and women are not afraid of risk and tend to take a fair amount of risk in pursuit of their goals even when there is a good chance that they may fail. They tend to be adventurous but not foolhardy.

Flexibility and scientific thinking Flexibility means being open to change and unbigotedly able to consider alternative views and options. Emotionally healthy individuals do not make rigid and absolutistic rules for themselves or others. They also apply scientific thinking to their own lives by reflecting on their emotions and actions and evaluating their consequences in terms of the extent to which they lead to the attainment of their short- and long-term goals.

Commitment A commitment to creative pursuits is a feature of emotionally healthy individuals. Such people tend to be healthier and happier when they are actively absorbed in something outside of themselves – and, without being fanatically devoted to their project or goal, manage to structure a good part of their daily existence around it.

Long range hedonism Well-adjusted people tend to seek the pleasures of the moment as well as those of the future, but they operate on the principle of long range hedonism, which means being willing to forego short term pleasures when these interfere with the pursuit of their more important long-term goals.

Responsibility for self Healthy individuals tend to accept full responsibility for their own emotional disturbances and will strive to overcome them using the methods of RET (as outlined in this book), rather than defensively blame others or social conditions for their disturbed thoughts, feelings and behaviours.

Non-Utopianism Healthy individuals accept that Utopias are probably unachievable. They also accept that it is unlikely that they will get everything they want and likely that they will frequently experience frustration and pain in their lives. Thus, healthy people refuse to strive unrealistically for *total* joy or perfect happiness on the one hand, or for a *total* lack or absence of anxiety, hostility, depression and self-downing on the other hand.

These, then, are our aims in writing this book. We suggest that you read through each chapter systematically and do the various exercises where indicated. Even if you do not feel that you are in the Comfort Trap, you can still help yourself to avoid it.

1

How and Why We Fall into the 'Comfort Trap'

How do you cope with discomfort in all its various forms? Notice that the question refers to *dis*comfort, not comfort; we do not normally experience difficulty coping with comfort! Nowadays, it seems, comfort is something people can't get enough of. How often do we hear people exclaim, 'Oh, I wouldn't feel comfortable doing this!' or 'I must feel comfortable before I tackle that!' and so on? The belief that one must be comfortable at all times entails certain consequences which often are far from comfortable. If we postpone taking appropriate action to resolve some problem, or to carry out some time-dependent task because we don't feel like doing it, we frequently find we have more difficult problems later. If we put off settling our bills promptly, we may incur hefty surcharges; if we delay making a start on repairing that leaking pipe in the attic, or put off taking our car in for an important service because it's a bit of a hassle, we can well pay a heavy price later for our procrastination.

Please understand we are not attacking comfort; we enjoy being comfortable as well as the next person. What we are saying is that if you allow yourself to be beguiled into believing that you must feel comfortable at all times and that life mustn't be too hard, you are likely, in the long run, to experience more *dis*comfort and hassle than if you were to forego some degree of comfort initially in order to feel more comfortable or at least, less uncomfortable, later.

There is no way that you can avoid frustration and discomfort so long as you are alive. Life today could well be spelt H-A-S-S-L-E. And since most people seem to believe – as we do – that it is better to live happily rather than miserably, our aim in writing this book has been to enable you to identify and eliminate certain major obstacles which seriously interfere with your ability to lead a happy and productive life. One of the most insidious of these roadblocks is the Comfort Trap. So let's take a closer look.

How and Why We Fall into the Comfort Trap

Human beings bring all kinds of desires to bear on whatever situation confronts them in life. We are born with desires. Without desires, and

5

the means to satisfy them, we would not survive. We are desiring beings. When our desires are met or satisfied, we feel pleasure, satisfaction, comfort. When our desires are not met, but frustrated, we experience irritation, displeasure, pain, discomfort. If we never experienced desire, we would never experience frustration or the discomfort arising from it.

The need for immediate gratification

When we experienced discomfort as an infant, we didn't put up with it for long. Possessing minimal tolerance for discomfort, our biggest asset at this point in our lives was a healthy pair of lungs and the ability to use them. As time went by we realized as we grew older that we received immediate gratification of our wants less and less frequently. We became aware of the fact that we often had to wait for what we desired. We realized that we had to develop tolerance of frustration at the same time as we began to understand the world around us, and that planned effort on our part was required more and more to satisfy our wants and needs.

However, we never cease to be fallible humans! Even as we mature and work to achieve our goals, we never really lose our desire for immediate gratification of our wants. We want what we want *now*, not tomorrow or the next day! It's nice to get what we want when we want it, to avoid discomfort and frustration as much as we can. It's *nice*, it's comfortable, but immediate gratification isn't necessarily rewarding or in our best long-term interests, as we will see presently.

The instant solution myth

Our technological culture does little to dispel the idea that we can all get what we want easily and quickly. An entire evening's entertainment can be enjoyed from the comfort of an armchair with no more effort than is required to press a few buttons on a convenient handset. Prepackaged already cooked meals for an entire family need only be placed in a microwave oven, the appropriate buttons pressed, and in no time the family dinner is ready for consumption. The highly successful credit industry has a slogan which epitomizes it all: 'Buy now, pay later'! As many unfortunate people are now discovering, the 'pay later' tag can entail serious consequences – the possibility of which may hardly have been considered at the time of purchase. In short, many powerful influences in our culture help to augment our short-range hedonistic tendencies to seek comfort and avoid frustration through offering us instant gratification now at the expense of greater cost, discomfort and anguish later. But, and it's a big 'but', we are not merely conditioned by influential elements in our society to think and behave in ways which are self-defeating. These elements don't *create* the widespread belief that we must have ease and comfort at all times; they merely exploit and take

6

full advantage of it. It is our own partly innate, partly acquired, tendency to think irrationally and to seek immediate comfort that causes the problem.

Fortunately for us, we also have the capacity to think rationally, scientifically, to ask questions and seek answers which make sense. We *don't have to* go along with the prevailing fads and fancies of the moment. We can challenge the slogans, the catchy phrases paraded before us. We began this chapter by stating our conviction that our purpose in life – which we believe is shared by most people – is to live happily. In other words, most of us want to have a long and happy life. In the context of our discussion of how we defeat our aims by subscribing to the philosophy of immediate ease and comfort, how do we go about the business of living happily for most of the 75 years or so we hope to have during our earthly existence? Let's see if we can come up with a rational alternative philosophy to replace the belief that we *must* always be comfortable, that life absolutely *should* not be too hard, and that we have to get what we want quickly and easily. In other words, what's the alternative to short-range hedonism?

Short-range hedonism

Short-range hedonism is the philosophy that our wants must be immediately gratified and that any discomfort we experience must quickly go away. As an example: Jane has been suffering from periodic toothache. She knows that a visit to her dentist is the answer but she keeps putting it off. Every time she thinks of making an appointment, she pulls back, and looks around for some distraction or pops a painkiller into her mouth. What do you think Jane tells herself just before she backs down from calling her dentist and making an appointment to see him?

Mainly, Jane is convincing herself: 'I know it's going to be painful because I need a filling and I know what that means! I *can't bear* the thought of all that drilling even if he gives me an injection! Maybe if I just hang on and use my painkillers the toothache will go away or not hurt me too much'. So, Jane opts out and succeeds only in reaffirming her belief that it's *too* painful to undergo a relatively brief period of sharp pain and discomfort. The result is that Jane perpetuates her conviction that she must not suffer discomfort and that an easier way out of her dilemma must exist. Jane is firmly locked in the Comfort Trap. Can you see how Jane's irrational convictions will not help her to solve her present problem, or others like it? Sooner or later, Jane's toothache will reach the stage where she is in constant pain. The cause of the pain in her tooth won't magically disappear. The longer Jane procrastinates over going to her dentist and getting the operation over and done with, the *more* pain and discomfort she will experience. In the end, she may have to have the tooth extracted or require a larger more expensive and more time-consuming filling than if she had seen her dentist as soon as she first became aware of the toothache.

The point is that when we avoid short-term discomfort, we actively invite long-term disadvantages which can often turn out to have serious consequences which we could have avoided by taking prompt action and putting up with the short-term discomfort in the first place. This is called low tolerance of discomfort or frustration, 'Low Frustration Tolerance' (LFT). 'Low frustration tolerance' springs from short-range hedonism and creates innumerable problems, as we will see later. One of the worst of these blights on one's life is procrastination, which gets a chapter to itself (Chapter 4).

Challenge the short-range hedonist philosophy!

The basic irrational belief (iB) underlying this philosophy can be expressed as follows: 'I must avoid, rather than face and deal with, many of life's difficulties and responsibilities since I need and must have immediate comfort and I can't discipline myself or suffer present pain to achieve future gains.'

The core idea here is that we must have immediate comfort. But can we rationally uphold that idea? It's OK to *prefer* comfort to pain (we're not advocating that you go out of your way to look for pain and discomfort; we're not great believers in mortifying the flesh, or suffering pain to purify one's soul) but where is it written that we *must* have immediate comfort? Is it realistic to demand it? Is the world revolving to make sure that we are comfortable, that all our wants are immediately granted and that nothing will be permitted to mar our bliss? Highly unlikely! And are we *really* so helpless that we can't discipline ourselves to put up with a predictable amount of discomfort and frustration which is the daily experience of practically all of us? When you claim that you can't stand something are you saying that you will literally come apart at the seams? If you can answer 'Yes' to any one of these questions you will be unique, for no one has done so yet, or is ever likely to!

If you feel you are in the Comfort Trap, you can help to free yourself from it by practising over and over again the techniques for disputing the irrational ideas which keep you in the trap as set out in the paragraph above. Once you convince yourself that these ideas cannot be upheld logically and that they have no connection with reality, you will find that their hold over you will weaken and give you leeway to begin *acting* against them. For example, you could start by forcing yourself to engage in some worthwhile activity which previously you had convinced yourself was too difficult to carry out without repeated attempts, or involved some degree of discomfort. Face the discomfort! Stay with it until you make yourself more comfortable. Work out what it would take to carry out the desired action, then, unrebelliously, push yourself into doing it, and continue doing it until you succeed at it. If the task is still presenting you with difficulty, break it down into more easily manageable chunks; you don't have to do it all in one go!

Your aim in challenging and disputing the irrational ideas which underlie short-term hedonism is to convince yourself that it is a self-defeating philosophy and to replace it with a set of rational alternative convictions which will help, rather than hinder, you in accomplishing your main goals in life.

The rational alternative to short-range hedonism

For convenience, we have highlighted the basic irrational belief which we introduced above and which, as we saw, creates and maintains short-range hedonism:

- 'I must avoid, rather than face and deal with, many of life's difficulties and responsibilities since I need and must have immediate comfort and I can't discipline myself or go through present pain to achieve future gains.'

In response to your challenges to that basic irrational belief, you could believe:

- 'I certainly prefer comfort but I don't *have* to have it.'
- 'There is no reason why I cannot face and deal with life's difficulties and responsibilities. In fact, I have every reason to do just that, because they are not going to magically disappear and they may well prove to be even more difficult to deal with if I were to avoid tackling them now.'
- 'Disciplining myself to carry out difficult or boring tasks may at times be hard, but it isn't *too hard*. If I want to enjoy the future advantages to be gained from dealing with some of life's difficulties now, I would be wise to accept the temporary loss of comfort as worth it in the long run. I won't enjoy the discomfort or the hassle but I can certainly stand it.'

Once you convince yourself of the validity of these more rational formulations, you will find your outlook and attitude to life more in keeping with the philosophy of 'long-range hedonism'. Let's see how it compares with short-range hedonism.

Long-range versus short-range hedonism

Let us say you are someone who seeks to obtain pleasure and avoid pain *and* to live a fairly long healthy life. You are constantly faced with choices. Suppose you are fond of fattening foods. You can indulge yourself eating chocolate, ice creams, pizzas and various pastries and get a large amount of pleasure from doing so. But if you also desire to keep your body healthy, to maintain a trim and fit appearance, you have to make a choice. You are faced with the choice of either going for the pleasure of the moment and enjoying your ice creams and pizzas, or severely curtailing your intake of these foods and substituting other, less fattening foods which won't add unnecessary pounds to your body weight. If your goal is to remain fit and healthy you have to discipline yourself to take appropriate measures to achieve it; and self-discipline, in turn, requires a high level of frustration and discomfort tolerance. In other words, you have to spring the Comfort Trap.

In the preceding section we offered advice on challenging and disputing the irrational beliefs which underly short-range hedonism and keep you in the Comfort Trap. We also offered rational alternatives to these irrational beliefs. If you can convince yourself of these rational alternatives you will, in effect, have replaced the self-defeating short-range hedonism with long-range hedonism which will give you a much better chance of getting the best deal you can out of life. Long-range hedonism says that if you accept some inconveniences in the present you will increase your chances of a happier and more productive life in the future. If your fancy runs to ice creams, pizzas and so on, as a long-range hedonist you allow yourself to experience the discomfort of not having what you would like to eat today in order to have the physique you would like tomorrow – and many other tomorrows. You will recall the case of Jane who put off going to her dentist, because she believed she couldn't stand the discomfort of having a filling. Jane could more wisely have decided to accept the discomfort of an early visit to her dentist to have her toothache attended to promptly for the advantages of maintaining a clean and healthy mouth in both the immediate and longer-term future.

We have laid considerable emphasis on the wisdom of sacrificing present pleasure for future gains. However, we are definitely *not* advocating that you continually sacrifice the present for the future. It's one thing to sensibly recognize that if your top priority is, say, to lose weight and to have and maintain a good physique, then that takes precedence over your liking for ice creams and pizzas, and that therefore you had better behave accordingly. But long-range hedonism does not exclude going to parties, entertaining friends, attending discos and so on. It merely means that *at times* you choose to deprive yourself of some immediate pleasure or comfort because you recognize it as having minor importance compared to the importance of attaining more desirable long term goals.

Major forms of low frustration tolerance

'Low frustration tolerance' and the Comfort Trap take several different forms. It is important to be aware of these variations, to recognize them when you are faced with them and to know how to deal with them. Let us emphasize once again why it is important to raise your level of frustration tolerance. We are not claiming that it is good for your character to suffer pain or discomfort uncomplainingly, or that you deliberately court pain and discomfort. Rather, by developing a high level of frustration tolerance you will be able to get more of what you want out of life and less of what you don't want. In a nutshell, that is what it's all about. So, let's move on now to a consideration of the major forms that LFT takes.

The experience of painful emotions

When you have an emotional problem, for example anxiety, which can be quite painful, you can regard that as a form of frustration or discomfort and consequently have low tolerance for emotion. You then tell yourself, 'I can't stand feeling this way!' That then often leads you to try to avoid the experience of anxiety if you can, or to exaggerate the feeling. You tend to go out of your way to avoid situations in which you have been anxious before or situations you think you are going to feel anxious in. You therefore deprive yourself of the opportunity to face up to your fears. People in this situation start off by being afraid of something and then they become afraid of their feeling of anxiety and will seek to avoid it. Similarly, you can become depressed about your depression, because you are saying to yourself:

    'I am depressed'
    'I can't bear feeling depressed!'
You then jump to the conclusions such as:
    'I'm always going to feel this way!'

Believing that, you frequently begin to feel hopeless and suicidal.

Challenge your irrational beliefs!

The way out of that situation where you have a problem about a problem is to focus on the irrational belief (iB) which is blocking you from dealing with the primary problem. In this instance you challenge and dispute the iB, 'I *can't stand* feeling this way!' The purpose of this is to show you that you *can* stand the feeling of anxiety or the feeling of depression. Once you realize you can stand your feeling of anxiety (for example) and are in fact tolerating it, you are then more able to deal with it, to face the things you are anxious about. If the problem is depression, you learn to cope with feeling depressed in order to deal with whatever it is that you are depressed about. Thus, if you have low tolerance of your upset emotions, this will interfere with your progress in resolving them. As we indicated above, tolerance is developed by challenging and disputing the irrational beliefs (iBs) which create and sustain your low frustration tolerance. You would therefore proceed to challenge and dispute these iBs as follows:

'I can't stand *feeling this way!'*
Dispute: Do you really mean that? You can stand anything until you are physically unable to do so. If you mean, 'I don't like feeling this way', that is probably true; we can always verify that. But where is the evidence that you literally can't stand a feeling? Your statement doesn't make sense because you are standing it; if you were truly unable to stand it, you would not be able to say anything whatever about it!

By contrast, the *rational alternative belief* makes sense and will help you to deal effectively with the basic problem. Thus, you could rationally believe:

• 'I'll never like feeling anxious, but obviously I can stand it.'
• 'By accepting that I have an anxiety problem and that it is an inconvenience, but hardly a horror, I can focus on ways of overcoming my problem instead of wasting my time and energy on feeling miserable for having the problem.'

You can tackle the irrational belief, 'I can't *bear* feeling depressed!' in the same way as it is saying the same thing.

'I'm always *going to feel this way!'*
Dispute: How does it follow that because you are depressed *now*, you will *always* be depressed? You cannot foretell the future so you cannot sensibly claim that you will always be depressed. Words like 'always' and its opposite, 'never' are usually gross overgeneralizations when applied to human behaviour.

A rational alternative to the irrational conclusion, 'I'll *always* be depressed!' would be:

• 'I am depressed now but there is no reason why I must go on being depressed indefinitely. I have not always been depressed in the past, I am merely depressed now, in the present. Since depression is something which I have clearly demonstrated I've lived without in the past, I can logically conclude that there is at least a possibility that I can live without it again'.

You could further reinforce your rational beliefs by repeating to yourself several times a day:

• 'Yes, it may be hard for me to change but I'd better face the fact that it's much harder if I don't. For then I'll keep my anxiety or depression and what good will that do me? So it's hard to change. But it will be even harder on me if I don't!'

Once you convince yourself of that and accept that it may feel uncomfortable at first when you start to change, but that you can certainly stand the discomfort, you are in a much better frame of mind to deal with the original problem.

We hope you can see now how unhelpful LFT can be and how important it is for your emotional health that you learn to control it rather than let it control you. Low frustration tolerance not only generates procrastination but by keeping you in the Comfort Trap interferes with your dealing effectively with any other emotional problems that may arise to trouble you.

Low tolerance for hard work

This is a second major form of LFT and it shows up in practically every area of life. It is particularly evident in some work-related area where a person is confronted with a task which involves hard work but which is in that person's interest to do. Preparing a report for your boss, or presenting a thesis for the award of a higher degree, are examples of time-limited tasks which can involve fairly hard work leading to some desired goal. Two other typical examples are: committing yourself to completely redecorating your house, inside and out, and undertaking, under medical advice, a strict diet and physical exercise schedule to achieve a target weight over a period of three months.

You want to succeed, you know it's in your interests to succeed, but you balk at having to do the necessary work to enble you to succeed. Or, believing that you shouldn't have to work too hard or overcome too many problems to get what you want, you may make a start on your particular task, but your efforts tend to be half-hearted and ineffective. Procrastination takes over and the task is abandoned sooner or later because of low tolerance for hard work and the demand for immediate gratification.

13

We will now examine the main iBs which generate those unconstructive attitudes leading to low tolerance for hard work:

'It's *too* hard!'

'It *must not* be hard!'

'I *should* only have to do it once!'

'It *must* be easier than it is!'

'It's too hard!'

Dispute: What does 'too hard' mean? If it means that present resources are inadequate for the task, then try breaking the task down to manageable chunks. If you still claim it is too hard but admit that it can be done, then 'too hard' cannot be accurately defined. You can legitimately claim that it definitely is hard work to resolve an emotional problem. That is a provable statement. But if something can be done, then to argue that it is too hard is really a meaningless remark. 'Difficult' or 'very difficult' can be given an accurate rating on some appropriate scale. But where does 'too hard' fit on the scale? Nowhere, we suggest.

'It must not be hard!'

Dispute: We have agreed that it is hard. So does it make sense to claim that it must not be hard? Obviously, if it is hard, it should be hard! We may wish that it wasn't hard but if it is hard, then it's hard and it makes no sense to claim at the same time that it must not be hard!

'I should only have to do it once!'

Dispute: This one is a favourite among those who believe that life must be easy. Difficult issues, they believe, can be and should be resolved by waving a magic wand.

If some work-related problem could be accomplished at the first attempt then it would not normally need more than one attempt. But the reality is that the type of work-related tasks we are discussing are not usually accomplished at the first attempt – or even the second, or third! Like it or not, hard work involves repetition and we had better accept it. Can you see that this irrational belief is similar to the one which holds that something shouldn't be hard when it is clear that it indubitably *is* hard?

'It must be easier than it is!'

Dispute: We hardly need to repeat what we said in our answers to the above iBs. If something isn't easy, it isn't easy. Once again it makes no sense to claim that a thing must be different from what it actually is.

You will not be surprised at this stage to learn that 'I must be

14

comfortable' frequently raises its ugly head in connection with low tolerance for hard work.

For example:

'I have to be comfortable in the moment!'
'I must be comfortable (before I start)!'

Dispute: Well, good luck! You might wait a long time! Comfort when performing some task usually comes *after* you have done the task, and quite often only *after* you have done it many times. You are in the Comfort Trap if you insist on being comfortable before you undertake the task. A variation of this iB is to say, 'I must be in the mood first' before you get down to actually doing whatever you want to do. If you propel yourself into making a start on the job, you very often then get in the mood and can go on under your own momentum. And even if you don't get into the mood you don't have to be in the mood in order to do something. The demand for 'comfort first' is a typical component of LFT, and because it virtually puts the cart before the horse it seriously interferes with your ability to do what you know intellectually you had better do, but which you foolishly insist you must feel comfortable about *before* you actually do it.

What are the rational alternatives?

Provided you have convinced yourself that the iBs above are illogical, unrealistic and lead to self-defeating behaviours such as procrastination, inertia and more pain and discomfort rather than less, you will now be ready to replace these unhelpful beliefs with more rational beliefs. Your aim is to minimize needless pain and discomfort and to enjoy your life – not to waste it in the Comfort Trap.

Thus, instead of these iBs we have just disputed, you could decide to hold these rational beliefs (rBs):

- 'Overcoming my problems may be difficult because doing so demands work but it isn't too hard. If work is what it takes, then I'd better work. I won't resolve my problems by waiting for some magical answer to turn up. There is no magic.'
- 'Self-improvement requires hard work. That is the way it is. I'd like it to be easy but it doesn't have to be easy. In fact it's silly to say it must not be hard when it obviously is hard. So I'd better buckle down to it and work until I have reached my goal. After all, that's what I really want.'
- 'I realize that only repeated effort and practice will help me to get where I want. Indeed, it would be nice if I could do it only once but there's no reason why this must be the case. I would be foolish to

imagine that just doing an exercise once will result in any lasting improvement. Doing it once is just the beginning!'

- 'Real change is not easy to accomplish. Longstanding habits don't just vanish overnight. So I'd better assume that making the changes I want to make is not going to be easy, nor is there any reason why it must be, although of course, it would be nice if it were easy. But it isn't!'

- 'I'd like to be comfortable in the moment but there's no law which states that I have to be comfortable. I am unlikely to feel comfortable when attempting something new or difficult for the first time. But if I work at it I can gradually become more comfortable and the more often I carry out my task the more comfortable I will tend to feel about it.'

- 'It follows from the statement above that if I wait until I feel comfortable before I start on my task, I could end up waiting forever! It would be nice if I could magically feel comfortable before I do something that involves discomfort but magic doesn't have to exist. In deciding to wait until I feel comfortable before I begin a task when it is clear that comfort comes only after I have made many attempts, I am putting the cart before the horse. If I always allow myself to wait until I feel comfortable before starting out on some new task, I'll be caught in the Comfort Trap forever.'

There's no easy way to spring the Comfort Trap. Changing unhelpful habits requires self-discipline plus hard work and practice at understanding, contradicting and acting against one's irrational and magical belief systems.

Let's take a practical example to show you what we mean by that. Let us suppose that you are reading this book because after glancing through it you thought it might be useful in helping you to break some habit or pattern of behaviour which is holding you back from living a more satisfying life. Perhaps the problem is procrastination, or perhaps you want to make a major change in your life but feel you can't face the discomfort and uncertainty entailed in actually going ahead and doing it. So you start reading this book and quite soon you think: 'Ah, this book will give me the insight I previously lacked. Once I see what caused my problems and learn how to change the way I think about them, I'm practically there! This is just what I need!' Sorry, but we're going to disillusion you! A third major form of low frustration tolerance which you will recognize as akin to low tolerance for hard work is:

Low tolerance for following thought with action.

A deep reluctance to disturb one's comfort and actually *do* something effective to resolve one's problems is typical of those who wish to solve their problems from the comfort of an armchair. These armchair problem solvers apparently subscribe to the irrational belief: 'Insight alone should be enough!'

If just reading this book could magically dissolve problems of procrastination, lack of self-discipline and all the other 'demons' which keep people in the Comfort Trap, the publishers would be charging a lot more for it! Luckily for the book publishers, perhaps, there is no shortage of armchair would-be problem solvers. Sadly, many people cling to the notion that once they see how their problems originated, that insight alone will somehow resolve them. That's what we mean by believing in magic. When, alas, the problems still persist and fail to disappear in spite of the insight one has acquired, a common reaction is to tell oneself, 'Hm, maybe I need more insight, dig a bit deeper down. That should do the trick!' And off they go to the bookstore to purchase another book . . . and another. It's so much *easier* isn't it, to reach an intellectual understanding of your emotional blockings than to actually *do* something effective to unblock yourself. Of course insight into the true nature of your problem is important, but it is only half the battle. Insight alone can even be something of a two-edged sword. For if you keep chasing after more and more insight while still taking absolutely no action specifically designed to undo your emotional blockings, you will still be faced with the problems you started with. Eventually you lose heart and become convinced that it's too hard to change, that some things cannot be changed, and that you might as well just stay as you are. Acknowledging your problems is fine; obtaining insight into how you created them is even better. But persistently working to uncreate and extinguish them is better still.

Three techniques for overcoming inertia and becoming actively involved

Challenging and disputing beliefs

We have already met these thinking techniques in the previous section. Study them again.

Go over them again and again until you know them so well that you can accurately recall each iB, the way you were shown how to dispute it and its rational alternative belief without having to refer to the book. In addition to these iBs you can add the following one to your list:

'Acquiring insight alone into my problems should be enough to resolve them!'

Dispute: There are three questions you can ask of any belief:
   is it logical?

is it realistic?

does it work?

It would be nice if insight alone solved our problems but does it logically follow that because it would be nice, that therefore it should? Can you come up with any logical reasons why insight alone should work?

If insight alone should be sufficient to enable us to overcome problems, then it would be. But is it? Suppose you read and understood how internal combustion engines in an automobile worked. Would that insight alone enable you to step straight into a car and start driving it correctly? If it were so, all you would ever need to do to learn to drive would be to read a book on driving. Do you think that idea is realistic?

Is insight alone going to work for you? Try it and see! For example, you know it's uncomfortable to alter your usual routine and start out, say, to look for a complete change of job although you admit it would be in your long term interests to do so. But you keep putting off doing something about it because it does involve a degree of inconvenience and discomfort. You know *why* you are procrastinating, but will that insight alone impel you into action? If it doesn't, then the belief that it will is wrong.

The rational alternative to 'Insight is enough':
● 'I would like to think that achieving insight into my problems would in itself be enough to resolve them, and that hard work wasn't necessary, but that isn't the case, and it doesn't have to be. Therefore I'd better accept that if I want to resolve my problems there is nothing for it but work and practice. I may not like it, but I can certainly live with it.'

Imagery

Let's suppose that you are anxious about undergoing an operation. A specialist has advised it, and although you accept the specialist's advice that it is in your best interests to have the operation done soon, you put off arranging a definite date. You are fearful about the outcome. You experience uncomfortable sensations and thoughts as you imagine yourself being wheeled down a hospital corridor and into the operation theatre: What if something goes wrong on the operating table! What if I still feel pain when I come out of the anaesthetic!'; 'I couldn't bear that!' you tell yourself.

And so you deal with this uncomfortable situation (the impending operation) by pushing the thought of the operation out of your mind and, temporarily at least, you feel more comfortable.

But, you know that you ought to go through with the operation for your own sake, and that the longer you postpone it the more difficult it could become. You want to get it over and done with but you hold back from making a commitment because of your anxiety about the outcome. So, in addition to the thinking techniques we suggested you could use to help yourself overcome your tendency to avoid discomfort, what else might you do to help yourself to go ahead and arrange to have the operation? Here is one such technique: It is called Rational–Emotive Imagery or REI for short.

As vividly as you can, imagine yourself in the hospital and about to be operated on. You've had the 'pre-med' and now they're wheeling you in to the operating theatre. Let yourself experience, intensely, the feeling you normally experience when you think about this situation. Let yourself feel very anxious as you imagine the scene. Now, stay with your feelings for a few seconds. Then, having keenly felt the fear and anxiety, *force yourself* to change this feeling in your gut so that you *ONLY* feel keen concern and sorrow, but *not* fear. You *can* force yourself to do it! Remember, feel only concern and sorrow as you visualize yourself in the same situation. If your upsetting feelings do not change as you attempt to feel more appropriately, keep imagining the same unpleasant experiences and keep working at your gut feelings until you do change these feelings. *Remember: you create and control your feelings, therefore you can change them.* Keep working at it! Once you no longer feel anxious, or fearful but only concerned and sorry as you are about to undergo the operation, note *how* you made the change from feeling anxious to feeling only concerned and sorry. What did you tell yourself to *make* yourself have these new appropriate feelings of concern and sorrow?

In order to change your feelings, you changed your beliefs about your situation in some manner. Let yourself see clearly what important changes you made in your belief system to create these new feelings about having the operation. Repeat this process. Make yourself feel anxious; then make yourself feel concerned but not anxious; then see exactly what you did in your head to change your feelings. Practise doing this over and over again. Keep practising until you can easily imagine yourself having some unfortunate experience, such as being about to undergo an operation, changing your feelings of anxiety or fear to feeling only concern and sorrow, and see what you do to change your belief system which creates and maintains your feelings. If you keep practising this REI for ten minutes every day for a few weeks, you will get to the point where whenever you think of going in for your operation – or indeed, experiencing any other unpleasant event whether or not it actually transpires – you will tend, easily and automatically, to feel appropriately concerned, sorry or displeased, rather than emotionally upset.

At this point someone might ask: 'Why do you suggest we change feeling anxious about going into hospital for an operation to feeling only concerned and sorry about it?' 'What's the advantage to be gained from going through all this rational-emotive imagery etc. if we end up just feeling concerned and sorry?' Our answer to this is as follows.

First, we can hardly expect you to say to yourself, 'Oh, goody! I'm going to be operated on!', nor would we want you to go to the other extreme and feel indifferent about the operation. You are being realistic if you accept that nothing can be taken for certain in life. It is highly probable that a given operation will turn out successfully. But because nothing can be predicted with certainty, there is always a small probability that some unforeseen circumstance will arise, or some post-operative condition will be discovered, which will complicate matters and necessitate a longer period of recovery following the operation, or even a further operation. Therefore, it is rational to be concerned about the possibility that things might not turn out as you would wish.

Second, anxiety is an unpleasant feeling. It causes needless pain. Concern, by contrast, is not such a painful feeling. Third, while anxiety inhibits us from acting to resolve some unpleasant situation, concern will strengthen our motivation to do something constructive to resolve the problem. You will take whatever steps you can, for example, to help matters go smoothly for you while you are in hospital. Also, you can legitimately feel sorry about the inconvenience involved. If you have young children, you may have to make arrangements for them to be looked after while you are away. If you have a business, you may want to arrange for someone to keep an eye on it for you, or you may even have to close it down until you are able to take control once more. In short, concern and sorrow are appropriate responses to your situation because they enable you to take a realistic view of it, they don't cause you unnecessary pain or discomfort and they motivate you to deal constructively and decisively with the problem rather than dither or procrastinate over it.

Rationally, you would be telling yourself something like: 'What a bother this is! I shall be inconvenienced by being in hospital for a time and possibly have to put up with some discomfort. Well, too bad! I won't like it, but I can certainly stand it. Since I'm advised to have this operation, it had better be done. So let me arrange it. The sooner it's done and over with, the sooner I'll get back to my own important pursuits and activities.'

If you vigorously and persistently practise this REI exercise for ten minutes each day for two or three weeks you will tend to convince yourself that discomfort is *only* inconvenient, *not* unbearable. Once these rational ideas begin to really sink in, your tolerance of frustration

20

and discomfort will increase, and you will find you can undertake previously 'fearful' experiences, like going into hospital, without feeling unduly anxious or panicked about it.

Together with the disputing techniques we showed you in the previous sections, these REI exercises will begin to develop your 'emotional muscle' to enable you to break out of the discomfort-avoiding habit and to take more control of your life. Finally, to tie it all together, we now describe some behavioural techniques – things you can *do* – to strengthen still further your new coping skills.

Self-management procedures

This technique is useful to 'get you going' when you balk at doing some task you know it would be wise to do promptly but which you resist doing because it requires an effort to get you started. You can use self-management techniques, for example, to help you carry out the disputing and rational-emotive imagery exercises.

Select some activity which you enjoy, something which really gives you pleasure. The performance of this pleasurable activity is then made contingent upon your doing the exercise. In other words, once you have carried out your exercise in disputing your iBs or your REI exercise, then – and only then, you 'reward' yourself by doing whatever it is you particularly enjoy. However, do ensure that the pleasureable activity you select is consistent with your long-term aims. For example, if one of your long-term aims is to lose weight or to get yourself into trim for running in a marathon, it would be unhelpful to reward yourself with generous helpings of cream cakes! Select instead some non-fattening but legal pleasurable activity.

If that doesn't work, you can penalize yourself – *not* punish or damn yourself – but give yourself some unpleasant or onerous task to perform immediately after each time you fail to carry out your assigned exercises.

This use of immediate rewards or reinforcements for carrying out these important self-help exercises coupled with the employment of strict, quickly enforced penalties, can work very well if you are seriously interested in overcoming problems of low self-discipline, LFT and procrastination.

2

'I Must Have What I Want!'

As long as we remain alive we, as humans, will have desires. If we didn't have desires we would probably not survive. It is healthy and life-preserving to have desires. Without the basic biological desires for food, shelter, safety and sex, few, if any, animals, including us, would exist.

However, once we get beyond the stage of mere subsistence and have more or less of a sufficiency of our basic survival needs – food, water, shelter and clothing – we begin to want all sorts of other things as well. No longer are we content with mere survival. We want more, lots more! Indeed, there seems to be no limit to the things we desire. There is nothing necessarily wrong with that. The problems begin when we realize that our resources are limited and that many of our desires cannot be met, either now or in the foreseeable future. The result is that many of our desires are frustrated.

How do you feel when your desires are not met? Normally you will feel disappointed, irritated, inconvenienced or sorry. That's how most people would feel. You wanted X and you got nothing. You've been deprived and you don't like it. But you tolerate it. You realize it's not the end of the world, so you try to find a way of getting what you want. If it turns out that it's still not feasible, you accept the fact and look for some alternative.

When 'I want' becomes 'I must have'

As we've just seen, desiring is healthy. Lack of desire or 'desirelessness' appears to us to negate human existence. So, if we just stay with desiring, it would appear that the worst that can happen to us (with some important exceptions) would be the occasional, but alas, inevitable frustration of at least some of our desires, and the consequent feelings of sorrow and disappointment. The important exceptions – such as being struck down by some serious illness, or the death of some loved companion, or suffering some other significant loss – would, of course, result in feelings much stronger than just sorrow or disappointment; you could legitimately feel extremely sad and sorrowful should any of these misfortunes befall you.

Unfortunately, we humans don't just stay with desiring: *we escalate our desires to demands*. We are not content with wanting what we want; we demand and insist that we absolutely *must have* what we want because we want it, or because, we tell ourselves, we 'deserve' it! And because the world does not always give us what we insist we must get, the result is a great deal of unnecessary woe and unhappiness.

Since our purpose is to minimize unnecessary unhappiness, let's take a close look at various forms of demandingness and see how they diminish our ability to enjoy life, and in fact, land us in the Comfort Trap.

I must get what I want

There are three directions in which this *'must'* missile can be launched:
   – at other people
   – at life conditions
   – at oneself.

Since our main focus is on discomfort anxiety, we shall deal only with the first two above; the third one, at oneself, causes a different kind of problem known as 'ego anxiety' which, put simply, results from demands made upon oneself (see Chapter 4, pp. 60–4). Both types of anxiety may be present and can interact as we will see later.

Demands made on other people

'I *must* get what I want because I want it. It's terrible if I don't get what I want; I *can't stand* being deprived of what I must have and you are a rotten person for depriving me and deserve to roast in hell!'

Demands made on the world in general or life conditions

'I *must* get what I want because I want it. It's terrible if I don't get what I want; I *can't stand* being deprived of what I must have, and the world is a rotten place for allowing it to happen!'

Anger and frustration of demands

Both examples above illustrate anger arising from low frustration tolerance. The demands are the same in each case, as are the damning conclusions. In the first, anger is directed towards another person or persons; in the second, anger is directed towards life conditions or the world in general. Note that whenever you make unconditional demands upon someone and damn that person when he or she fails to meet your demands, the resulting emotion is anger. You feel angry, and maybe the other person will feel angry back – for being damned for not acceding to your wishes.

Now, the goal is to get rid of disturbed feelings, that is to say, feelings which are needlessly painful, which motivate us to behave in self-defeating ways, and which block us from achieving our goals in life. We term these feelings 'inappropriate' because they interfere with our basic purpose in living – to stay alive and live healthily and happily with our chosen relationships over a good number of years.

Consider anger for a moment. How well do you think anger will help you to achieve your goals? Initially, bullying and cursing others may cow them into obeying your demands, but only temporarily. In the long run, your anger-inspired tactics will probably boomerang and defeat you. Who would want to live with a dictator? Disturbed or inappropriate feelings, as we will demonstrate throughout this book, spring from irrational ways of thinking about oneself, other people and life events or conditions. Depression and anxiety are other good examples of disturbed feelings. Nobody enjoys feeling really depressed or anxious, and when you are feeling depressed or anxious you don't feel motivated to tackle energetically the problem you are depressed or anxious about. As a result, you tend to stay depressed or anxious, you don't progress towards your goals, and time, of which there is nothing more precious, is wasted. And again with anger, when you express anger towards someone, you may feel good momentarily; anger is often linked to a conviction of righteousness when you verbally let fly at somebody who has violated or flouted some rule you personally deem important. But as your anger flares and adrenaline is pumped into your bloodstream and your blood pressure builds up and you feel tensed up all over, you won't feel good then. There is also the disruptive effect of your anger on your relationships with other people (for more on anger, see also Chapter 3, pp. 48–51.)

On the other hand, so-called negative feelings such as sorrow, regret or annoyance are healthy, appropriate reactions to negative life-events. Why do we term them 'appropriate'? Well, first, these feelings spring from rational ways of viewing these negative life-events. For example, suppose you lose something you value such as a good job, or a close relationship with someone. Both of these occurrences would be regarded by most people as a negative life-event. If you were to experience one you would feel neither happy nor indifferent about it. If you thought rationally about your loss or misfortune, you would feel sorry, regretful, or disappointed, because it *is* disappointing when you lose a good job you wanted to retain, and it *is* a matter for regret or sorrow when a valued relationship with someone breaks up. You are clearly disadvantaged and inconvenienced by your loss and therefore your feelings of sorrow, and so on, are appropriate.

Further, when you feel only sorry or disappointed, rather than depressed or anxious, over a job loss or relationship breakup, you tend to stir yourself to go out and find another job or try to get back with the person whose relationship with you had broken up if you think there is a chance of mending it. *Appropriate feelings are healthy and self-motivating.* They serve your best interests and help you get what you want out of life. *Inappropriate* feelings do the opposite.

That is why we target disturbed or inappropriate feelings, such as anger, depression, and anxiety for change. Inappropriate emotions spring from rigid, inflexible irrational beliefs, particularly when these are expressed in the form of absolute demands. On the other hand, healthy emotions spring from rational beliefs, that is to say, beliefs which are non-dogmatic and flexible and express preferences rather than demands and which are logical and realistic. It follows, then, that if we wish to change disturbed feelings, we need to modify the thinking processes which create them. Specifically, we need to uproot our irrational beliefs and replace these with rational alternative beliefs. 'We feel as we think'.

Dispute: Disputing something involves asking and answering questions:

1. Where is the logic in saying: 'Because I want something, I must have it'? Suppose you said: 'I want a sunny day tomorrow for our picnic, therefore I must get it'. Does it logically follow that you will get a sunny day because you demand it? Because you *want* something to happen it is not logical for you to believe that therefore it absolutely *must* happen. When you link a 'must' to a preference you are into magical thinking. If magic did exist then all you would have to do is to want something for it to be yours.

2. Is it consistent with reality to say: 'Because I want X, I *must* get X'? If there was a law of the universe which said that you must always get what you wanted, how could you possibly fail to get it? The world would have no option but to obey you. The reality is that the world operates according to its own laws, not yours or ours. Since there is no law which decrees that you must get what you want because you want it, it makes no sense to believe that there is such a law. So if you believe that you must get what you want just because you want it, you've invented that law yourself, and you would be wise to repeal it and stick to reality: the universe obeys only its own laws.

3. What is meant by: 'It's terrible if I don't get what I want'? You could prove that you are inconvenienced or disadvantaged when you don't get what you want. But 'terrible' means more than being inconvenienced; it means 100 per cent bad. Can anything you could ever experience be so bad that it couldn't possibly be worse? 'Terrible' is a word which is used very loosely nowadays. If you really mean that it is 'terrible' when you don't get what you insist you must have, you are going beyond the bounds of reality and escalating a disappointment into a catastrophe. Being slowly crushed to death under a pile of fallen masonry following an earthquake with rescuers powerless to reach you may strike you as near to being as terrible an experience as anyone could have. But even here

there are degrees of pain. Some may be pulled out dead after a few hours under the rubble, while you may be rescued only after ten days of unremitting pain. No matter how bad a thing can be, it can always be worse! So let's not make things worse than they are by 'terribilizing' what are really only disadvantages or inconveniences of varying degrees of unpleasantness.

4. The belief: 'I can't stand being deprived of what I must have', is typically expressed whenever one is frustrated or thwarted. Since it really means that something is regarded as unbearable, this is clearly an example of a gross exaggeration. If you really couldn't stand something, you would come apart and be unable to say anything! Without exception, no person who has told us: 'I can't stand X–Y–Z' has ever died from X–Y–Z. No one we ever knew disintegrated as a consequence of being deprived of something he or she demanded that he/she must have. Exceptionally, a person who is going to die unless he or she is administered some special life-saving drug can validly claim that they couldn't stand being deprived of it. But the great majority of us can stand being deprived of many things we think we can't stand being without. The fact is that we can stand anything until we expire.

Another meaning people attach to 'I-can't-stand-it' is the belief: 'I can never have any happiness again!' Is this a provable statement? Since no one can predict the future, the statement can neither be verified nor disproved. It is an example of 'Always or never' thinking. Or, put another way, it means that a given belief has either zero or 100 per cent probability of being true. Apart from death itself, can you think of anything in human life which can be labelled certain to happen or certain not to happen?

5. Isn't damning somebody to roast in hell for refusing to grant you your wishes something of an over-reaction? Or is the world necessarily a rotten place because it doesn't grant you your wishes? Even if everyone agreed with you that you had been treated badly, how does that make the person responsible for treating you badly a total scoundrel who deserves to suffer forever? Are people *only* their behaviour? Is that all there is to being human – just your acts and traits? Is that all *you* are? People behave badly towards us because of ignorance, stupidity or malice. Will damning these people make them behave better? Maybe they can be helped to act more considerately but there is no evidence that damning them will encourage them to change their obnoxious ways; rather the reverse is true. They will tend to behave worse.

Will damning the world as a rotten place when the world doesn't immediately grant you your wishes make any difference? You don't run

26

it, so why should it accede to your wishes? The world doesn't owe us anything and damning it for being the way it is won't change it and we will only give ourselves a needless pain in the gut if we persist at it.

Assuming that you can see why demanding and expecting things of other people and the world involve irrational and unsustainable convictions, what rational philosophies could you come up with to replace them?

The rational alternative to 'I must get what I want'

Rational beliefs (rBs) are flexible, non-dogmatic, logical and realistic. They express preferences rather than demands. They make sense. Thus, you might like to compare the irrational beliefs:

> 'I must get what I want because I want it . . . and you are a rotten person for depriving me . . .' and 'I must get what I want because I want it . . . the world is a rotten place . . .'

with the following rational alternative beliefs.

Rational alternative:

- 'I definitely prefer to get what I want, but I don't have to. If I fail to get what I want, this is unfortunate and disappointing but hardly terrible. I can certainly stand the disappointment although I'll never like it. If other people or my life conditions frustrate me by depriving me of what I want, that is too bad, but neither other people nor life conditions need be damned as rotten on account of it. Maybe I can calmly figure out a way to get what I want more often in future.'

'I must get what I deserve'

The idea that we should get what we deserve, and its sister idea that we should not get what we don't deserve, are widely believed. As children we are taught that if we behave as we are told and do well, the things we want will eventually come our way because we deserve them. As adults, many of us still believe that if we behave well, act kindly to others, work hard and conscientiously and so on, then one day we will be rewarded by having our own wishes fulfilled because that is what we deserve. A nice thought, perhaps, but is it true? We personally know individuals who complain bitterly to anyone who will listen to them, about how unjustly they have been treated by their families, their relatives or the world at large. The usual refrain is, 'I've been hard done by. After all I've done for them, this is all I get in return!'

If you believe that you must get what you think you deserve, or that you mustn't get what you think you don't deserve, you are in the Comfort Trap. You legitimately believe that because you are intelligent and hardworking you will usually or probably achieve at least some of the things you strive for. There is no guarantee that you will, but the chances are that you will succeed more often than if you just sat back and did nothing. But you cannot show that *because* you have worked hard and persistently and have been driven by the desire to succeed that therefore the universe *owes* you success. For if that was the case, you would *always* succeed.

If you believe that the universe has some obligation to reward you in some way because you have worked hard, been kind to people and so on, you may fall for the idea that you deserve a little comfort now, and that having done enough to deserve something in return for all your hard work, you can now relax and wait for the reward you 'deserve' to come to you, rather than continue to strive for the attainment of your goals. Then when achievement of your goals still eludes you and you begin to realize that you are not going to get what you think you deserve from life, you feel upset.

We need hardly labour the point that life isn't fair. There is no perfect justice or deservingness in the world. In some places you would be hard put to it to find even *im*perfect justice! It would be wise, therefore, to try to stop thinking in terms of deservingness for two reasons: first, because the idea is unrealistic, and second, because it creates unnecessary emotional pain and unhappiness.

The basic irrational belief behind the idea of deservingness is:

'I must get what I deserve' and its twin 'I must not get what I don't deserve'.

Why do we contend that this belief is irrational? There are certain criteria or tests you can apply to determine whether a belief you hold about yourself, other people or life conditions is rational or irrational. We mentioned these earlier and now put them in an easily understood format (see Table 1).

Now let's apply these criteria to the belief, 'I must get what I deserve'. Better still, let's make it more specific. Let's suppose that you have worked hard and saved money over a long period to buy yourself and your partner a holiday home in a pleasant sunny part of the world which you both regard as an ideal place to retire to eventually.

Then, one day you are appalled to learn that the bank in which you had invested all your savings has gone bankrupt. Your hard-earned savings have gone and you are unlikely to get back a penny in compensation.

You feel depressed, angry and hurt. You tell yourself, 'They absolutely should not have treated me in this unfair manner. It's terrible to be treated in this way, particularly as I *do not deserve it*. Poor me! The

Table 1 Features of irrational and rational beliefs

Irrational beliefs	Rational beliefs
Unrealistic, i.e. make no sense, not factual.	Factual, make sense/consistent with reality as determined by a consensus of objective and intelligent judges.
Illogical, i.e. self-contradicting, or the conclusions do not follow from the premises.	Logical, i.e. the conclusions follow from premises.
Block people from reaching their goals, and demotivate them.	Help people achieve their goals and motivate them to overcome obstacles.

---

world is a rotten place for allowing this to happen. They are no good for treating me in this way.'

The feelings of depression, anger and hurt are real enough. Many people would agree that they would be bound to feel the same way if a similar thing happened to them. But there is also another way of looking at it.

First, let us see why the ideas expressed and the emotions you experienced in response to this financial debacle will be unlikely to help you feel better about your misfortune or help you to recover your losses. Let's apply the criteria we set out in Table 1 to the beliefs you hold about your misfortune. We shall group them in the same order as they appear in the table.

• *Is my belief realistic?*

The first part says, 'They absolutely should not have treated me in this unfair manner.' But it obviously did happen. If it should not have happened, if some law existed that did not allow it to happen, then it wouldn't have happened. Moreover, the bank is run and staffed by fallible human beings and there is no law of the universe which says that the bank must be run competently. It doesn't *have to* be run competently. The owners and staff can even choose to run it badly – or even fraudulently! They have that choice. So, the belief is unrealistic.

• *Is my belief factual?*

Granted that the loss of money was very unfortunate, is it really 'terrible', meaning as bad as bad can be? Is that factual? Can you maintain it is the worst thing you could imagine happening?

• *Does my belief make sense?*

29

You conclude that because you do not deserve to be treated unfairly, 1. the world is a rotten place for allowing it, and 2. they are no good for treating you in this way.

Consider 'The world is a rotten place for allowing it'. If you think about it, the world has no control over everything in it. While some individuals somewhere presumably had some control over the bank, those individuals are fallible human beings like the rest of us. Perhaps they knew about the state of the bank's finances; perhaps they didn't. But even if someone had total control and responsibility for the viability of the bank, that person is no superhuman or god but merely a fallible human who can only do his best but who cannot *guarantee* that investors will be protected against every conceivable calamity. There are no guarantees.

Next, your belief: 'They are no good for treating me in this way' implies that the bank, or some people in it are no good at all, and are totally without any redeeming features for not having looked after your money. Even if deliberate negligence or fraud could be proved against some person or persons, the fact of their acting badly or criminally does not make them totally worthless, but only fallible humans whose actions have caused harm to others and who had better be arrested and made accountable in law for their misdeeds.

● *Is my belief logical?*

No. The belief is illogical because there is no reason why the fact that you do not desire to be treated unfairly means that you absolutely must not be treated unfairly. As we stated peviously, when you link a 'must' to a preference or desire you are into magical thinking. Few of us want to be treated unfairly but in spite of our wishes, we quite often are. That is a fact of life. So it does not make logical sense to believe that because we don't like the way certain things are, therefore they must not be the way they are.

● *Can I prove 'deservingness'?*

What about my belief that 'I do not deserve it'? Who can say what we 'deserve'? You can legitimately hold that because you have worked hard, are intelligent enough to realize that investing your savings in a bank is usually a more sensible way of making your money grow than risking it on the result of a horse race or some other gamble, therefore you are likely to receive some return. But you cannot logically show that because of your hard work, your prudence and desire to own a holiday home, therefore the universe undoubtedly *owes* you a return on your investment – or indeed anything, for that matter. If that were the case, you would *always* get what you were owed. Since that kind of obligation or necessity clearly doesn't exist, your belief that you don't deserve to be treated in the way you were treated is obviously illogical and therefore irrational.

● *Does my belief help me achieve my goals?*
So long as you feel in a damning and self-pitying frame of mind you are unlikely to motivate yourself to take constructive action to minimize or overcome your loss. You are more likely to think of ways of getting even with the perpetrators of your misfortune to whom you attribute mischievous intent. Or, in your self-pitying mood, you may be inclined to give a ready ear to those who try to reassure you that 'the government will do something', and thus adopt a passive wait-and-see attitude to the problem of obtaining compensation.

If you agree that the beliefs and attitudes we've outlined above are irrational, what do you think would constitute a rational alternative set of responses to the same problem?

A rational alternative to 'I must get what I deserve':
● 'I prefer to be treated fairly, or at least, not unfairly, but there is no reason why I must be treated in the way I prefer regardless of what I may think I 'deserve'. Obviously I don't have to get what I think I 'deserve' or don't 'deserve' and although it is bad to be treated in this way, it isn't terrible. As for the bank, I definitely don't like their behaviour but they are only fallible humans who have acted badly and they are not damnable or worthless creatures for having acted so.'

If you held a set of rational beliefs similar to these, how would you then feel about your misfortune? You would feel very disappointed and annoyed about the way you had been treated. You would feel motivated to instigate action to recover some of your lost money or obtain some kind of compensation. Realizing that you were not the only investor with the bank, you might consider teaming up with others similarly affected to try to obtain some legal redress from the bank or its owners, or the courts. Without the drawbacks of anger and self-pity you would stand a much better chance of communicating your feelings and wishes clearly and assertively to the bank or the relevant authorities concerned with it, and maybe improve your chances of minimizing your loss and obtaining compensation.

'I must have certainty!'
It would be nice to know sometimes how a decision or an action is going to turn out. There would be obvious practical advantages to knowing in advance whether something you want to achieve will in fact be achieved. That is a healthy desire. It expresses a preference and you can produce reasons for it. 'I prefer to know if such-and-such will work' is rational. Note, however, you cannot be certain, that is, 100 per cent sure. You can

get very close to it in some instances, but never absolutely certain.

The irrational beliefs here are:

'I *have to* be certain' or, what amounts to the same thing,

'I *can't bear* uncertainty'.

What does 'I can't bear uncertainty' really mean? It means I can't bear the *discomfort* of not knowing for sure what the outcome of some action is going to be. That is why the demand for certainty puts one firmly in the Comfort Trap.

This demand for certainty can lead to paralysis in decision-making: 'I have to be certain before making a decision' leads to indecision. For, if you have to be certain of the outcome of a course of action before you make a decision, you will never make the decision because you cannot be certain. The following story illustrates this point:

This donkey was dying of thirst in the desert. At last, it came to a crossroads. It remembered that one path led to a clean water well, the other path to a well where the water was rancid. The donkey knew that it could just about survive on the rancid water but it could not remember which path led to the rancid water and there were no signposts. The donkey wanted the clean water but it *had to* be certain of which path would lead it to the clean water. Once it set off there would be no turning back. It simply *had to* be certain before it decided which path to take. What happened? The unfortunate donkey died at the crossroads. There was no way it could be certain which direction led to the clean water, so it was unable to make any decision.

Paradoxically, low tolerance for the discomfort of uncertainty explains why people sometimes act impulsively or rashly: they have to be certain before they make a decision; since they cannot be certain before they make a decision, and because they cannot tolerate the discomfort of not being certain, they break the impasse by taking a decision impulsively.

Well-meaning friends or colleagues do a disservice to people with a low tolerance for uncertainty. By offering reassurance and trying to persuade these people that their decision will turn out all right, in spite of the uncertainty, the decision-maker is denied the opportunity to face the uncertainty and learn to tolerate it.

The demand for certainty can take many forms. Here is a realistic example of an irrational belief which underpins the demand of many people for 'certainty':

'I must be certain of success before I undertake any hard work that is necessary to enable me to resolve my problem.'

Dispute: You may wish you could be certain of success but is it logical to insist that because you want something to be the case, therefore it *must*

be? Aren't you really demanding a guarantee of success before you begin? Are there any guarantees that we will succeed because we want to succeed? If guarantees of success existed then wouldn't we always succeed? Wouldn't we be bound to know of them? We know of none ourselves but if you find any, please let us know!

If there are no guarantees of success isn't it unrealistic to demand them? Maybe an all-powerful being could guarantee us any desired outcome but so far we have not yet made the acquaintance of one. Also, think how dull life would become if we could always be certain of how everything would turn out! Can you imagine living in a pre-programmed robot world? Variety may be the spice of life but uncertainty is the driving force which makes both life and variety possible.

Demanding certainty of success before you tackle some task is not going to help you achieve your goals if no certainty exists. In fact, if you demand to be certain of success before you decide, you will never decide!

The rational alternative to the demand for certainty:

- 'I would prefer to be certain at least some of the time that my efforts to reach certain goals would turn out exactly as I wished, but I don't have to be certain. If hard work is necessary to achieve my goals, then I would be wise to accept that that is how things are. At least some of the time I may never like the uncertainty of not knowing if my hard work will turn out successfully, but I can live with the uncertainty.'

'I have to be in control'

This demand is closely related to the demand for certainty. Many humans have difficulty in accepting the idea of randomness. In one way this dislike or fear of randomness or unpredictability has been beneficial. It inspired the search for knowledge and understanding of nature which is the mainspring of science. If humans had never been curious about how nature worked, science would never have arisen. Primitive religion is in its way an attempt to understand how nature works and to exert some kind of control over it. Science and technology aim to do the same thing but from very different theoretical standpoints, and by and large they have been very successful.

However, the iB 'I *have to* be in control at all times' is irrational for several reasons.

Dispute: Does it logically follow that because I want to be in control, therefore I must be? It is OK to want what you want but does it logically follow that because you want or desire something, therefore you absolutely must be granted it? If that were true, then whatever you desired would automatically be granted. The 'must' would see to it! Now obviously no such logical necessity exists and to believe that it does exist puts you in the realm of magic.

Is it consistent with reality, this belief that you must be in control? 'Must' doesn't mean maybe or just sometimes. It means necessarily and always. If you must be in control, you have to be in control. It means you have no choice about it. It would be a law of nature and you would have to go along with it. You would like to be in control? That's OK, a legitimate wish. But it is totally unrealistic to believe that you *must* be in control when clearly there is no such law.

Do you believe that being in control at all times would help one to achieve one's goals? 'I must be in control!' you repeat to yourself. But look at what happens when you demand that you must be in control at all times. When you are not in control you experience anxiety about the dreadful things you imagine could happen because you are not in control. Then you get control. What happens then? Does your anxiety disappear? Not at all! You begin to worry then about losing control. As your anxiety over this dreaded possibility builds up, you increase the chances that you will lose control. When you do eventually lose control – since realistically, one cannot be in control at all times – you are back where you began: you are miserably anxious when you are not in control, and miserably anxious about losing it when you *are* in control!

In what way, therefore, would always being in control help you towards achieving your goals? The answer is, It wouldn't!

The dire need to have everything under control is the mainspring of 'discomfort anxiety'. People who suffer from discomfort anxiety find it difficult to accept that one cannot eliminate risk or uncertainty from life. In a sense all life entails risk from the moment you come into the world until the moment you leave it. To overcome discomfort anxiety you need to accept that the demand for control at all times is irrational because it's impossible.

The rational alternative to 'I have to be in control'

- 'I prefer to be in control of my life as far as is practical, but I don't have to be in control. Not being in control at all times may be somewhat disadvantageous to me, but it isn't terrible and I can obviously stand it. I can accept that there are limits to what I can control and while I may never like it I can live happily in spite of it.'

If you subscribe to these rational ideas your anxiety over not being in control at all times will tend to diminish. You may also find you tend to get on better with other people. People who convey the attitude that they must be in control all the time can be difficult to live with. If you drive a car, you will know what a nuisance a back-seat driver can be: they can never relax and let go; they constantly distract your attention and lower your concentration on driving; they have to be in control even when they're not.

'I must feel confident before I do it'

This irrational demand is similar to the demand, 'I must be comfortable before I begin', which we discussed in Chapter 1. The iBs which we identified and disputed there, together with the rational alternative beliefs are virtually identical. If you simply substitute 'confidence' for 'comfort' as you do the exercise, you will find the comparison instructive. As was true with the demand that one must feel comfortable before carrying out some task or activity, you are in the Comfort Trap if you insist on being confident before you tackle some task or carry out some activity. Confidence, like comfort, comes after you have carried out the task, or performed the activity, usually several times. The old adage, 'practice makes perfect' could be expanded to 'practice leads to confidence and comfort comes with practice'. But if you insist on waiting until you feel comfortable or confident before you tackle something, you could wait forever!

> Lisa F. wanted very much to learn to drive, but she couldn't bring herself to start taking driving lessons. 'I must feel confident when I'm driving and I couldn't feel confident learning to drive in the kind of traffic there is on the streets nowadays', she explained. 'Before I drive a car in that traffic I've got to be confident I can do it properly', was her response to all suggestions that she undergo driving instruction.

In Lisa's case, anxiety over what people would think of her if she performed badly while driving, underlay her demand that she must feel confident before she took a car on to the road. Once she was shown how unnecessary and self-defeating her (ego) anxiety was and eventually succeeded in replacing it with rational concern, she came to realize that she could build confidence bit by bit by practising driving under qualified instruction and overcome her discomfort anxiety by actually driving in heavy traffic and tolerating the discomfort. Lisa eventually passed her test and accepted that there was really no other way she could have acquired the confidence to drive safely and comfortably in all kinds of traffic.

Strictly speaking, you can not claim to be confident about doing something you have never tackled before. You can say, 'I know how to do this because I've done similar things before', but until you actually do it you cannot assert that you are confident you can do it. Confidence comes with doing, which is why work and practice are necessary if you wish to overcome your problems. Suppose you had a problem with procrastination. Insight alone may show you *how* your problem may be resolved, but not until you actually do the exercises, and succeed in overcoming your procrastination can you say: 'I'm confident I can overcome procrastination because I have already done so'.

3

'I Can't Bear Feeling This Way!'

One of the unfortunate things about feeling anxious or depressed is the unwillingness of those who suffer in this way to acknowledge their feelings. People will say: 'I can't bear thinking about my depressed feelings', or 'I can't bear this feeling of anxiety I get when I go up for my annual appraisal interview'. The reason why it's unfortunate is that people don't solve their problems with this attitude; in fact, as we shall see, they make their problems worse. As a result, these people go through greater discomfort than if they had faced and tackled their problems when they first became aware of them.

When anxiety is a problem

If you feel anxious about something but are avoiding doing anything constructive to resolve it, you may feel anxious about being anxious! You may be telling yourself, 'I *mustn't* be anxious!', or 'I *can't* bear feeling anxious!' As a consequence of holding these negative evaluations about yourself, you will tend to behave in ways which provide you with temporary relief from the discomfort you feel when you acknowledge to yourself that you are anxious, but which make it even more uncomfortable for you in the long run. Thus, you try to block off the discomfort you experience whenever you acknowledge your anxiety by such manoeuvres as:

1. Avoiding situations that provoke anxiety. Since any number of situations could theoretically trigger off your anxiety, you tend to lead a restricted life – perhaps a *very* restricted life – as a consequence.
2. Carrying out rituals to ward off anxiety – e.g. wearing a certain tie, or carrying out some daily routine in a strict order.
3. Using 'tricks' such as trying to convince yourself that it doesn't matter if you lead a restricted life or if you lose out on a number of life's pleasures, when you believe deep down that it really does matter.
4. Abusing drugs: you may for example, overindulge in alcohol, or increase your cigarette smoking, or even take up smoking when you previously had been a non-smoker.
5. Avoiding anxiety-provoking thoughts by practising various distractions – e.g. going out shopping when you don't really need to, or rearranging your furniture or doing some non-urgent household chore.

Anxiety about anxiety leads to the avoidance of anxiety-provoking situations, but this serves only to reinforce your anxiety. For example, in a social situation if you think it is terrible to be anxious in that situation, one of two outcomes are likely: either you don't go to it and thus reinforce the idea that it would have been terrible if you had gone. Or, you do go to it, but anxiety about your anxiety typically leads you to drink too much. You don't approach anyone. You go on drinking. You observe that nobody is paying you any heed. Everybody is too busy laughing and chatting away to the people beside them. So you stay silent and eventually leave. You realize you've had a miserable time and then you tell yourself, 'You see, it's no good! I must avoid this situation in future'. In fact what you have done is to create a self-fulfilling prophecy. It goes like this. A socially anxious man typically believes: 'People don't want to get to know an uninteresting person like me. Why should anyone find me attractive?' Truly believing in his own basic worthlessness, this man actually behaves as if he were worthless: he keeps to himself, avoiding eye contact with others, and if there happens to be a bar, he will usually be seen with a glass in his hand, gazing around at no one in particular. Not surprisingly, such unsocial behaviour does not invite approaches from others. The man then interprets and evaluates this lack of response from others as proof of his own worthlessness: 'I was right. People don't really want to know me. I really am no good.' Thus this individual perpetuates his problem of social anxiety.

Janice was a case in point. Like the man in the example we've just provided of a self-fulfilling prophecy:

Janice suffered from ego anxiety (EA). A shy, pretty, girl who lived a rather quiet life, she had been to one or two parties but hadn't enjoyed herself. She felt awkward at them. She didn't know what to talk about. She tended to avoid getting into conversation with others and felt everybody was looking at her when she occasionally opened her mouth to say anything. She thought people would be criticizing her for not dressing stylishly like the other girls, or making fun of her behind her back because she didn't have a boyfriend. As a result, Janice tended to avoid invitations to parties, and the like, because, as she explained, social situations 'make me anxious'. She might have added: 'And I can't *bear* feeling anxious!', for she also had the problem of discomfort anxiety (DA). And her discomfort anxiety reinforced her problem with ego anxiety.

One day, Janice met an ex-school friend, Jenny, in the street. Janice and Jenny had always been good friends. 'Hi, Janice! What are you doing Sunday evening? We're having a barbecue at my place, 7 O'clock onwards. Why don't you come along? You'll have a good time!' Janice thought Jenny would think it rude of her to refuse the invitation, so she said she would be there.

As Sunday drew nearer, Janice felt more and more anxious. She had never been to a barbecue. She wondered what she should wear; would she look 'right', should she bring any food or drink? Janice wondered if she should call her friend and ask her what to do but decided not to. She thought she would look foolish by asking such questions. In her mind, people invited to barbecues should *know* what to bring with them and what to wear!

Sunday duly arrived, and Janice was greeted at the door by her friend, Jenny. 'Hi, Janice! Glad you could come! Here, meet Joey and Frances, make yourself at home!' Janice just nodded politely to Joey and Frances, then made her way to the garden where the barbecue party was in full swing. Janice noticed the food sizzling deliciously on the barbecue. She would have loved to eat some of it but she couldn't bring herself to pick up a plate and join the queue. What if she was clumsy and forked a steak off the burner only to drop it on the patio? Just what would people think then of her? Horror! So Janice stood back and slowly sipped a small glass of the homemade punch someone had ladled out to her. When her friend invited Janice to help herself to some food, Janice excused herself by saying she didn't feel very hungry. Having hardly spoken to a soul all evening apart from the occasional 'Yes', or 'No', Janice returned home feeling thoroughly miserable. 'Never again!', she told herself, 'I'm just not cut out for that sort of social life. I feel anxious in social situations and I can't bear feeling anxious!'

Can you see that Janice's experience was another example of a self-fulfilling prophecy? She goes to the barbecue believing that nobody will find her interesting or will want to get to know her. She is also afraid of appearing gauche, of 'putting her foot in it', of what others will think of her. That's her ego anxiety. So she withdraws from active participation in the barbecue and since her unsocial behaviour does not invite approaches from others, she returns home convinced of her own worthlessness.

Janice's discomfort anxiety arises from the fact that she feels afraid not only of parties, barbecues and the like, but also of the uncomfortable feelings she predicts she will have when she thinks about, or is invited to these social functions. She avoids these uncomfortable feelings by pushing them out of her mind and refusing as best she can any involvement in future social functions of the kind she is afraid of. Fear of experiencing uncomfortable feelings associated with feared situations may, in extreme cases, result in fears of fainting, or having a heart attack. These fears act as further disincentives to resolving the primary problem of ego anxiety (see Chapter 4, pp. 60–4) and thereby help to perpetuate both ego anxiety and discomfort anxiety.

Overcoming anxiety about anxiety

When you feel anxious about being anxious, look carefully at what you are telling yourself to create this problem about a problem. Virtually all upset feelings are created by the irrational ways we think about and evaluate the events in our lives. We explained in Chapter 2 how disturbed or inappropriate feelings stem from irrational beliefs (iBs), and how iBs could be identified behind various kinds of inappropriate feelings? Read that chapter again if you think you need to refresh your memory. There are also iBs which make us feel anxious about being anxious.

When anxiety about being anxious is bothering you, look for the irrational beliefs (iBs) which underlie the *secondary* problem, that is to say, the anxiety *about* anxiety. The primary problem is your original anxiety, that exaggerated fear of some event or circumstance which you perceive as a threat to your self-worth. This is usually a form of ego anxiety. [For advice on how to deal with this form of anxiety, read our book *Think Your Way to Happiness*, Sheldon, 1990.] The secondary problem of anxiety *about* being anxious is a manifestation of discomfort anxiety, which is the main focus of our attention at the moment.

We are dealing with the secondary problem first because if you can overcome your secondary problem (about being anxious), you will then be in a much better position to find out what is causing your primary anxiety problem. Usually, this will be some form of ego anxiety which is best dealt with separately.

Since we are dealing with discomfort anxiety the main irrational beliefs we are looking at now are:

'I *must not* be anxious!'
'Anxiety is *terrible!*'
'I *can't bear* being anxious!'
Dispute:
'I *must not* be anxious!'

Why *mustn't* you be anxious? It would be better for you if you were not anxious. But because it would be better for you not to feel anxious, does it follow that you mustn't be anxious?

Moreover, if you are anxious, you are anxious. It makes no sense to demand that you must not be what you are. What rational Belief (rB) would be a preferable alternative to the iB 'I *must not* be anxious'?
Rational alternative belief (rB):
- 'I strongly prefer not to be anxious but there is no law of the universe which says that I mustn't be anxious. If I'm anxious, I'm anxious, but I can accept myself as a fallible human being with my anxiety.

Dispute:
  'Anxiety is *terrible!*'

Granted it is uncomfortable and sometimes painful to be anxious, but does it logically follow that it is terrible? Used properly, 'terrible' means much, much more than merely uncomfortable. It means just about as bad as anything can be. Is that true about anxiety?

Rational alternative belief (rB):
- 'Anxiety is certainly uncomfortable and disadvantageous to me socially because I will miss out on many potentially pleasureable activities through avoiding social functions because of my anxiety. But anxiety isn't terrible, it's only an inconvenience, a nuisance and therefore only a problem which can be tackled and resolved.'

Dispute:
  'I *can't bear* being anxious!'

You say, 'I can't bear to be anxious!' Well, you could have fooled us! Here you are alive and sounding like a normal human being, so what do you mean when you say that you can't bear being anxious? If you literally couldn't bear something you would collapse or come apart at the seams! Yet you are in one piece. Obviously you *can* bear being anxious, because you are bearing it!

Moreover, when you say, 'I can't bear being anxious', you are implying 'And I'll *never* be happy again!' How could you prove that you'll *never* be happy again? Even if you remained anxious for the rest of your life, does it follow that you could never be happy under any circumstances? You might not be *as* happy as you could be without anxiety but do you really want us to believe that you could never ever again know any happiness? That is highly unlikely! The words 'never' and 'always' had better be used very sparingly if you value mental health and rational living, because these words as commonly used very often are simply gross exaggerations and inapplicable to human emotions.

The rational alternative belief (rB):
- 'I don't enjoy being anxious but I can certainly bear it. Since anxiety is an inconvenience and a disadvantage, I can view it as a problem to be dealt with rather than a horror to be upset about. There is no reason why I can't be happy with, or without my anxiety although I'd be less disadvantaged and probably happier without it. So I'd be wise to try to rid myself of anxiety and enjoy my life more.'

These disputes of the iBs behind anxiety about being anxious are examples of the kind of cognitive or thinking challenges you can make when you are confronted by some disturbed feeling you want to get rid of.

Another way you can combat secondary anxiety is to show yourself that you can tolerate the discomfort you feel when you are in an anxiety-provoking situation by actually entering such a situation, staying in it for a reasonable time and convincing yourself that it's only uncomfortable and not dangerous or terrible to be in the situation. Moreover, you don't leave the situation until you have overcome your original anxiety. In the case of Janice, for example, after she had convinced herself that the iBs underlying her anxiety about being anxious could keep her firmly in the Comfort Trap forever, and cause her to miss out on a lot of life's pleasures, she could be encouraged to accept invitations to barbecues and parties where she would normally experience social or ego anxiety, in order to show to herself that nothing terrible would happen to her, that no matter how uncomfortable or awkward she might feel, she could stand it, and that the discomfort would be bearable (and lessen with time).

Once she could tolerate the discomfort of being anxious, and was beginning to replace her previous self-upsetting beliefs with more rational convictions, she would then be in a better frame of mind to look into the irrational beliefs behind her primary ego or social anxiety. But until she was able to get over her anxiety about being anxious in certain situations she would lack the motivation to tackle her primary anxiety. That is the rationale for the emphasis in this book on discomfort anxiety. If you have a problem about a problem, tackle the secondary problem first. Once you accomplish that, you automatically give yourself a much better chance to deal successfully with whatever was your primary problem in the first place.

Anxiety about being anxious is underpinned by irrational beliefs. Once you are really convinced of the alternatives to these iBs, the rational beliefs outlined above, you lose your feeling of anxiety over being anxious. You might still be uncomfortable about your anxiety but the discomfort would motivate you to get down to tackling the primary problem of how you originally became anxious in social situations, and why you are still anxious in these situations.

In other words, once you succeeded in springing the Comfort Trap and could tolerate the discomfort of being anxious in social situations, you could then get down to tackling the basic problem of reducing or eliminating your life-restricting ego anxiety so that you could participate comfortably to the fullest extent you desired in these social activities you had previously avoided.

When you are depressed about being depressed

Feeling depressed is uncomfortable enough as anyone who has suffered from depression will readily testify. However, before you go any further, please note this important caution. Some forms of depression have a major physiological component and need the attention of a qualified physician. How do you know whether you are depressed in a clinical sense? Here are some signs:

- You feel hopeless about the future and helpless to do anything to ease your plight. You may even feel suicidal.
- You are preoccupied with failure and your own worthlessness.
- Your sleeping pattern is disturbed (too much or too little) and you especially wake early.
- Your appetite is disturbed (increased or decreased) with noticeable weight change.
- You have lost interest in sex.
- You feel fatigued, drained of energy.

If you think you may be depressed consult your doctor in the first instance. S/he will suggest appropriate antidepressant medication or make a referral for psychotherapy. You must deal with your major depression first, before you use this book. However, if your depression is mild and you don't have many of the symptoms mentioned above, this book will help you to understand and deal with your depression.

Unfortunately, some people become depressed about their depression and give themselves a double dose as it were. As we saw in the previous section, if you have a problem about a problem, the solution to the basic or primary problem gets overshadowed by the secondary problem. In effect, you are telling yourself, 'Oh my, I've got a problem of X and that's awful. I can't bear thinking about it. It's too uncomfortable. I'll just blot it out of my mind and do nothing about it.'

If you are depressed about some situation and then you become depressed about your prior depression you are probably telling yourself, 'I *can't stand* feeling depressed!' Believing that, your action tendency is to isolate yourself from situations which remind you of your depressed feelings. The restrictions you impose upon yourself lead you to feel depressed about your depression and you then say, 'I *can't stand* this feeling! It's hopeless, I'll never get anywhere!' As a result of clinging to these irrational Beliefs you'll stay depressed.

Being depressed about depression leads you to avoid tackling the issue of how you became depressed in the first place because it is uncomfortable; you can't bear feeling depressed, you can't bear thinking about it.

43

The way out of this Catch-22 situation is to examine and dispute the iBs which underlie your depression about being depressed. These iBs are similar in form to the iBs which create anxiety about being anxious and can be stated as follows:

'I *must not* be depressed!'

'Depression is *terrible!*'

'I *can't bear* feeling depressed!'

Dispute:

'I *must not* be depressed!'

You do not want to feel depressed because it is uncomfortable, but why *mustn't* you be depressed? It would be better for you if you were not depressed, but does it logically follow that because you don't want to feel depressed and it would be better for you if you were not depressed, that therefore you *mustn't* be?

Rational alternative belief (rB):

● 'I would certainly prefer not to be depressed but there is no law of the universe which says that I mustn't be depressed. If I'm depressed, I'm depressed. That's unfortunately how it is.'

Dispute:

'Depression is *terrible!*'

'Terrible' means 'awful', as bad as bad can be. Depression is certainly uncomfortable and unpleasant but is it so bad that nothing could be worse? Depression is bad enough without making it feel worse by making out that it's terrible.

Rational alternative belief (rB):

● 'Depression is uncomfortable and disadvantageous to me socially because I will miss out on many pleasurable activities through feeling too depressed to attend them. But depression isn't terrible, it's only very inconveniencing and painful and therefore a problem which can be tackled and resolved.'

Dispute:

'I *can't bear* being depressed!'

The fact is that you obviously *are* bearing it so it makes no sense to say you can't bear it. Telling yourself that you can't bear feeling depressed may only make your depression feel worse than it is.

Apart from being untrue, when you say: 'I can't bear to feel

depressed!', you are also implying, 'And I can *never* be happy again!' If
you think about it, doesn't that seem like quite an exaggeration? For
here you are making a forecast which, taken literally, means that for the
rest of your life you will never again know even a moment of happiness.
Can you really support that? You may not be feeling particularly happy
now if you are depressed, but does that prove that you can *never* be
happy? It doesn't! The words 'never' and its opposite, 'always' are
largely inapplicable to human emotions.

Rational alternative belief (rB):

- 'There is nothing pleasant about being depressed but I can certainly
bear it. Being depressed is a distinct disadvantage but I can view it as a
problem capable of being resolved rather than a tragedy to get myself
upset about. There is no reason why I can't be happy in future when
my depression is a thing of the past. So I'd be wise to take whatever
measures are needed now to rid myself of this depression and help
myself to lead a happier, more enjoyable life.'

Repeat the disputes of your iBs vigorously and persistently until you
really begin to see that they simply don't make sense. Practise disputing
your iBs until you convince yourself that you really no longer believe
them. In addition to working on surrendering your iBs by vigorously
disputing them regularly and frequently, you can reinforce your anti-
awfulizing disputing by giving yourself behavioural assignments – like
those Janice undertook to help her get rid of her anxiety about being
anxious. Thus you can force yourself to visit friends you have been
avoiding. If you have been avoiding them because being with these
friends triggers off memories of some situation you became depressed
about, you can convince yourself that it's uncomfortable to be reminded
of certain past events but it isn't awful or terrible and that you can stand it
because you are standing it.

Mark was a 37-year-old computer salesman who was made redundant
during the economic recession in the early 90s. This misfortune was
followed by one disappointment after another as Mark tried in vain to
find another job. There was simply nothing doing in Mark's particular
job market and to make matters worse, when he did get within sight of
some employment, he was often told at the interview that he was 'too
old'; they wanted younger men who could be trained in the new
technologies, not experienced but expensive salesmen who had done
well selling the hardware and technology of the previous decade.

After several fruitless months of job hunting Mark became
depressed. He abandoned the search for work, telling himself it was
hopeless to even try. His circle of friends began to shrink as Mark

withdrew from friends and colleagues he had previously worked with. He started drinking more than he could really afford and soon he had given up going to social events he had previously enjoyed attending.

Mark's depression sprang from the irrational belief: 'I absolutely should not have lost my job. And the fact that I can't get another job means that I'm no good.' Mark's loss of self-worth is typical of ego depression. Ego depression can occur because the person has a negative view of self. Thus Mark became depressed because he concluded that he was no good because he failed to find another job as he believed he should have done. Depression resulting from self-devaluation is called 'ego depression'. Unfortunately Mark's (ego) depression was accompanied by such acute feelings of discomfort about his (ego) depression that he refused to confront his depression and consequently continued to suffer. In other words, Mark's actual depression, plus his strong feelings of discomfort about being depressed, drove him into the depressive reactions of refusing to look for other work, avoidance of socializing and over-indulgence in alcohol. It was clear that Mark would be resistant to changing his depressed feelings so long as he remained horrified about the discomfort of continually feeling depressed.
Mark's irrational beliefs:
  'I *must not* be depressed!'
  'Being depressed is *terrible*!'
  'I *can't bear* feeling depressed!'
  'I'll *never* get another job and be happy again!'

These iBs represent the essence of all forms of discomfort disturbance, i.e., defining almost all one's strong wants as absolute needs.

When Mark was shown that he would remain depressed so long as he clung to these irrational beliefs, he was persuaded to examine and dispute them one by one in the manner outlined in the previous section. When Mark eventually saw that these iBs would keep him in the Comfort Trap and virtually ensure that he would remain depressed, his beliefs about his depression began to change towards more rational convictions. Thus he came to believe:

- 'I don't want to be depressed but I can see that it doesn't logically follow that because I don't *want* to be depressed, therefore I *mustn't* be. If I was omnipotent and could get whatever I demanded, I could just say, "Depression, be gone!", and it would vanish. But that's magical thinking and I don't believe in magic.'
- 'Depression is pretty bad but I can see now that bad doesn't mean terrible if "terrible" means being as bad as anything can be. I guess it

would be hard to find something that was totally or 100 per cent bad because things could always be worse.'
- 'I realize that uncomfortable though it may be, I can certainly stand being depressed. Uncomfortable doesn't equal "can't bear it", and although I'm unlikely to ever experience depression as anything but uncomfortable, I can certainly put up with the discomfort of it. In fact the sooner I do accept that depression is only uncomfortable and not a horror, the sooner I'll be able to tackle it head on and rid myself of it.'
- 'I can see now that believing I'll *never* get another job and be happy again is going over the top. I can think of all kinds of ways in which I could be happy even if I never worked again, and even that is questionable. This recession won't last for ever and life doesn't stand still. There will almost always be opportunities for people with brains and determination to get somewhere. So let me dump my silly catastrophizing about the future and go for it!'

The rational alternative to being depressed about depression

The aim of these exercises in disputing your irrational beliefs and the accompanying behavioural assignments is to contradict in thought and in action the irrational beliefs that you can't bear feeling depressed. In other words, they are intended to show you that you definitely can bear feeling depressed. For until you can do so, you will block yourself from being able to tackle the major irrational beliefs which brought on your depression in the first place. If you doggedly persist at doing these exercises you will tend to arrive at a new more rational philosophy which will probably be along the lines of:

- 'I would prefer not to feel depressed, but there is no reason why I must not feel depressed. If I'm depressed, I'm depressed.'
- 'It is uncomfortable to think about my depression and I wish it wasn't, but it isn't awful or terrible, it's just a nuisance.'
- 'It is certainly unpleasant to feel depressed but I can bear the discomfort of feeling depressed. If I could not bear it I wouldn't be around anymore! So obviously I can put up with the discomfort although I'll never like it.'

If you came to really believe something along these lines, you would rarely jump to 'It's hopeless' or 'I'll *always* be depressed!' because 'always' or 'never' thinking stems from being depressed about your depression and the irrational beliefs or cognitions that underpin it. You would also feel more motivated to get back to resolving the problem of how you depressed yourself originally.

Problems with anger

Right from the start let us make clear what we mean by anger. Many people confuse anger with annoyance. Anger typically occurs when some event of circumstance occurs which blocks one from achieving a valued personal goal or where some person or institution has transgressed some personal rule deemed important in one's personal domain. It is important to realize that your anger *isn't caused* when you are blocked from achieving a valued personal goal, or when somebody violates some rule or code of behaviour you deem important. You might well feel annoyed if either of these things happened to you, but you wouldn't necessarily feel angry. By 'angry', we mean furious, enraged. So what really causes anger?

The irrational beliefs behind anger

If for example, you infer that someone has deliberately treated you in a nasty, inconsiderate or unfair manner, it is not your inference that you have been badly treated that by itself accounts for your subsequent feeling of anger; rather it is the irrational beliefs (iBs) you hold about your inferences. Typically you believe:

'I don't like the way you are acting and therefore you *must not* act in this way!'
'And because you are acting in a way you *must not*, you are damnable for doing so!'

When you are angry, enraged or furious, you feel the physiological effects on your body and other people present notice those effects. Your blood pressure rises as adrenaline gets pumped into your bloodstream, your heart beats faster, you tense up. Annoyance doesn't have these effects to the same extent.

Now, some people have been brought up to believe that anger is not allowed. As children they may have been told that anger is sinful, or something like that. Not having been trained to understand how people make themselves angry as a result of their irrational beliefs about things that happen to them, these people become angry just like most of the rest of us. But because these people cannot feel they have 'permission' to express their angry feelings – because they have been taught that to do so is seen as sinful or shameful – they tend to conceal their anger in various ways.

Thus, either they avoid situations which they know or believe will provoke them to anger, or they mis-label their anger or even quash it altogether. An example of mis-labelling is when an individual responds to an action by someone else by being bitterly sarcastic towards that person for having allegedly behaved ineptly or unfairly. For example, if someone backs into your car and damages it the driver may be truly apologetic and about to offer you compensation, but you cut him off with: 'You're *sorry!*' you shout, 'You do hundreds of pounds worth of damage to my car by carelessly backing into me and all you can say is you're *sorry!* Don't you watch where you're going?' When a friend who was with you at the time asks you why you reacted so angrily, you reply, 'What? Me angry? I never get angry! I was only telling that idiot to be more careful in future!'

People who quash or deny their anger by mis-labelling it as: 'Just pointing out where someone went wrong' cannot bear to acknowledge their angry feelings because to do so would make them feel uncomfortable. As was true of anxiety and depression, the main problem of discomfort anxiety is that it stops you from dealing with the original problem.

Another form of anger-avoidance behaviour which is more subtle is fear of risk-taking. A person who can't bear feeling angry will avoid risking encounters with people whom he or she thinks might create an angry confrontation, even though it might be in that individual's better interest to confront assertively the person or people concerned. Believing that such situations would make them angry, and being unwilling to acknowledge their feeling of anger should it arise, these risk-avoiding individuals blame themselves for suppressing their anger and feel even worse as a result. They may even develop cardiovascular problems as a result of allowing their anger to go simmering on.

In order for people to be more accepting of themselves in anger, they need to first identify the irrational thoughts behind the anxiety about feeling anger. These would be along the lines of:

'I *must not* feel angry!'
'It's *terrible* to feel angry because it's unworthy of me and demeaning.'
'I *can't bear* feeling angry!'

Note the similarity between the iBs underlying each of the problem areas we have discussed so far! As we mentioned in the sections on anxiety and depression, the iBs we disputed there have a habit of turning up when you are confronted by some disturbed feeling you want to get rid of. See if you can dispute the above anger-generating iBs on your own and check your efforts against ours which follow below.

Dispute:
'I *must not* feel angry!'

49

No one wants to feel angry; anger has real disadvantages, including the risks to one's health. But does it logically follow that because you don't want to feel angry, that therefore you mustn't feel angry? Moreover, when you use 'must' or 'should' in the absolute sense, you imply that your wishes carry the status of dictates which the universe has to obey. If that were the case then you wouldn't be angry!
Rational alternative belief:

- 'I would prefer not to feel anger because anger carries real disadvantages including various risks to my health. But there is no reason why I must not feel anger. If I am angry, I'm angry.'

Dispute:
  'It's *terrible* to feel angry because it's unworthy of me and demeaning!'

Where is the evidence that it's terrible, i.e. 100 per cent *bad* to feel angry? Are there no worse things on the scale of badness than anger?

You claim that feeling angry is unworthy of you and demeaning. Doesn't this imply that you see yourself as above such mundane feelings as anger? Like everyone else, you are human and therefore subject to human feelings, failings and weaknesses. As for anger demeaning you, do you claim that feeling anger somehow magically makes you less of a person?
Rational alternative belief (rB)
- 'It isn't terrible to experience anger, only disadvantageous and self-defeating. Feeling angry may be bad for me and for others, but I am not a bad or worthless person for acting badly, only a fallible human being who doesn't like losing control.'

Dispute:
  'I *can't bear* feeling angry!'

It makes no sense to claim that you can't *bear* feeling angry, because you obviously are bearing it. You may not like feeling anger but you can definitely tolerate it.
Rational alternative belief:
- 'I'll never like being angry but I can certainly bear it, and provided I accept my anger as a problem I can deal with and not a matter to be horrified about, I may well find that I can substantially reduce my tendency to anger. The fact is I can learn to live with or without anger and to accept myself as a fallible human being even if I never entirely rid myself of my anger.'

Once you acquire this more rational attitude towards your problem of acknowledging your anger, you would then be in a much healthier frame of mind to undertake the problem of reducing or eliminating your anger by identifying and uprooting the irrational beliefs which create and sustain it.

'I can't bear feeling ashamed or guilty!'

Shame and guilt are two more examples of disturbed or inappropriate feelings which are basically problems of ego anxiety but which can generate discomfort anxiety which interacts with ego anxiety and thus makes the primary problems harder to resolve, at least initially.

Shame is the feeling we experience when a weakness of ours is publicly revealed and where we agree with others' negative view of ourselves, then denigrate ourselves for revealing our weakness. Guilt is what we feel when we have broken some personal code of morals or rule of personal behaviour and believe that we absolutely should not have done what we did, and that therefore we are despicable and deserve to be damned and punished.

The irrational beliefs behind shame and guilt

Shame

'I must not reveal my weaknesses in public, and I must not be disapproved of by others.'

'Because I have revealed a personal weakness in public, people will notice this and think badly of me.'

'If people notice my weakness and think badly of me, that makes me feel no good.'

Guilt

'I have done the wrong thing and I absolutely should not have done what I did.'

'Because I did what I absolutely should not have done, I am a sinner, a rotten person who deserves to be punished.'

Can you see why these beliefs are irrational? With regard to shame, you don't have to agree with other people's negative evaluation of you or denigrate yourself for displaying a fault or weakness. As for guilt, you may be guilty of performing a wrong act; that is a factual statement which may be verified. But when you feel guilty you are denigrating yourself for having committed a wrong act. In both shame and guilt the conclusion drawn in each case – namely, that there is something intrinsically bad or worthless about you – doesn't stand up to critical examination. In effect you are taking one or two aspects of you – usually items of behaviour

51

which you evaluate negatively – and then extending and over-generalizing these negative evaluations to the whole person. It's as though you're saying to yourself: 'I've made a mistake or have done the wrong thing. Now colour me *bad*!'

Once you denigrate yourself as a rotten person because of shame or guilt, you may come to feel so uncomfortable that you convince yourself that you can't bear feeling ashamed or guilty. The irrational beliefs (iBs) then become:

'I *must not* feel guilty or ashamed!'
'It's *terrible* to feel guilty or ashamed!'
'I *can't bear* feeling guilty or ashamed!'

As an exercise, try disputing these iBs along the lines shown previously, and then replace the iBs with your suggested rational alternative beliefs.

The rational alternative to 'I can't bear feeling ashamed or guilty'

- 'There is no reason why I must not feel ashamed or guilty although it would be preferable if I didn't.'
- 'It is unfortunate if I feel uncomfortable about being ashamed or being guilty but it isn't terrible to feel this way. It's only too bad and a nuisance. As for my feelings of shame and guilt, maybe I'll be able to work on that problem once I stop making a holy horror out of the fact that I feel ashamed or guilty.'
- 'It is definitely uncomfortable to feel ashamed or guilty but it isn't awful and I can certainly bear it. I'll never enjoy feeling this way, but I can definitely stand it. And the fact that I can stand being uncomfortable will help me to face and tackle my original problem of shame or guilt.'

Marie was due to deliver a lecture to a fairly large audience of accountants on company taxation – a subject on which she had specialized. She had meticulously prepared her notes for the occasion and when it was Marie's turn to give her talk, she discovered as she laid her sheaf of papers on the lectern that these papers were not her lecture notes but a detailed shopping list for the coming week. Of her lecture notes there was no sign! Haltingly, Marie told her audience that she had mislaid her notes, and would they please excuse her for five minutes while she returned to the ladies' cloakroom to recover her notes which must be still in her handbag.

Blushing furiously as she overheard one or two ribald remarks from the audience and feeling deeply ashamed of herself for acting so ineptly before such an audience, Marie recovered her notes from her handbag and returned to the rostrum to give her talk. But by then she felt so upset that she gave her talk in a haphazard and unconvincing manner. Long before she had ended, her audience were yawning and shuffling their feet. Never had Marie felt so ashamed and she decided there and then to refuse any further invitations to give talks. 'I feel so ashamed', she told her friends, 'And I can't bear it!' she added.

Marie's feeling of shame was an example of ego discomfort. Her feelings of shame arose from the iBs behind shame and guilt (see p. 51). But Marie's acute feelings of discomfort about her shame were responsible for her decision to avoid all further involvement in public speaking. The iBs behind Marie's decision to avoid further engagements were virtually identical with those we outlined above:

'I *must not* feel ashamed!'

'It's *terrible* when I do feel ashamed.'

'I *can't bear* feeling ashamed!'

Marie overcame her discomfort over feeling ashamed by challenging and disputing the iBs sustaining her discomfort and replacing them with the rational alternative beliefs.

Marie's rational alternative beliefs to 'I can't bear feeling ashamed!'

- 'I would prefer not to feel ashamed when I act stupidly in public but there is no reason why I must not feel ashamed. If I feel ashamed, I feel ashamed.'

- 'It isn't terrible to feel ashamed, it's just a nuisance and I don't like it but I can live with it.'

- 'Who says I can't bear feeling ashamed? Obviously I can bear it because I did bear it. It's no great shakes to make a silly mistake in public but it isn't the end of the world and if some people in my audience think badly of me, that's their view but I don't have to make it mine. So maybe I'd better try to rid myself of this feeling I have of being ashamed when I goof in public. The sooner I do, the sooner I'll get back to public speaking and be able to enjoy it again.'

'I can't bear thinking this way!'

Some people believe it's horrible to think in a certain way. They tell themselves: 'If I think in a certain way that proves that I'm bad or worthless'. They then feel uncomfortable when they do find themselves thinking in the way they deem unacceptable. Noticing how uncomfortable they feel when these 'bad' thoughts assert themselves, these people then tell themselves over and over again: 'I *mustn't think* this way!' until they become so preoccupied with that thought that quite soon they develop a full-blown obsession about their 'bad' thinking. The result is that they think even more about what they originally tried not to think about.

This is an example of how ego anxiety and discomfort anxiety can interact to reinforce each other. The individual starts off by observing that he is thinking in a certain way which he deems unacceptable. He believes that he must not think that way, but because he does think that way, he condemns himself as worthless. At this point he experiences ego anxiety. Then because he feels uncomfortable at finding himself in this worthless state when he thinks bad thoughts, he demands of himself: 'I *mustn't* think this way!' At this point he feels discomfort anxiety. But the more he tells himself, 'I *mustn't* think this way!' the more he does think that way and back he goes to ego anxiety and then back to still more discomfort anxiety – the cycle repeating itself until the individual becomes totally obsessed about his thinking. The drawing below illustrates the point:

The iBs behind 'I can't bear thinking this way' may be understood by studying the following example of how an obsession about the possibility of going gay was treated.

In the discussion that follows we wish to make it clear that in no way are we implying that there is anything unacceptable about being gay or becoming gay or, for that matter, about being biased towards any other sexual orientation. An individual's sexual preferences are his or her own affair. The attitude of the counsellor is strictly non-judgemental in questions involving an individual's sexual orientation, and the job of the counsellor is to help the individual resolve any *psychological* blocks, or hangups which may be hindering the individual from freely choosing and following whichever sexual orientation he or she prefers.

'What if I'm gay!'

A young man whom we shall call Richard was on a teacher training course which was attended by a number of other men around Richard's age. Richard observed that he found some of his fellow male students attractive-looking. Richard found this thought alarming: 'What if I'm gay!' he wondered. The thought that he might be gay made Richard feel distinctly uncomfortable. This thought in turn led Richard to tell himself over and over again: 'I *mustn't think* this way, I *mustn't think* this way!' This in turn led him to think even more about being gay until he became quite obsessed about it. He tried not to look at men but the more he tried not to look at men the more he did look at them!

The way to undo Richard's obsession about going gay was to help him to change his thinking. Basically, Richard's iBs were:

'I *mustn't think* this way!'

'It's *terrible* to think this way!'

'I *can't bear* thinking this way!'

To change a belief you question it to find out if there is any truth in it.

Dispute: It may be undesirable (in Richard's case) to think that one might be going gay but does the fact of it being undesirable for him to think that way make it imperative that he *must not* think that way? Does it really logically follow that because something is undesirable therefore it absolutely must not exist? Richard agreed that his belief was illogical. Richard also saw that if something absolutely must not exist, there was no way that it could exist, and therefore his belief, 'I *mustn't think* this way!' made no sense.

It is merely uncomfortable (again in Richard's case) to think that one might be going gay but it isn't terrible. 'Doesn't "terrible" mean the same as 100 per cent bad?' Richard was asked: 'Can you really maintain that going gay can be equated with dying slowly with an incurable disease, or losing all your loved ones in an automobile crash?' He agreed that in terms of badness there was no comparison between his fears and these tragic outcomes.

Challenged to support his assertion that he couldn't bear going gay, Richard admitted that his assertion made no sense. After all, here he was standing what he said he couldn't stand. Richard eventually agreed that while he might not like the discomfort of thinking he was going gay, he could put up with the thought and could certainly bear the discomfort.

Once Richard realized that his beliefs about going gay were irrational, untenable and likely to cause him needless emotional pain, he began to think in more rational and self-helping, rather than self-defeating ways. In addition to his new rational beliefs, Richard began to put the whole issue into perspective.

- 'If I find myself thinking that some men are attractive looking, that doesn't necessarily imply anything about my sexual orientation.'
- 'I can unconditionally accept myself as a human being with value to myself regardless of who or what I find attractive.'

Once Richard succeeded in de-escalating his horror of thinking he might be gay and accepted that he need not condemn himself for thinking about men, and that even if he still thought men were attractive, that did not necessarily imply he was gay, or becoming gay, he stopped obsessing himself about looking at men and no longer agonized over becoming gay.

'I can't bear thinking or feeling this way because if I do I will harm somebody'

This type of thinking, as we showed in the previous section can also lead to obsessions. For example, an individual might be afraid to think about tube trains. He believes that if he thinks about tube trains he might think of throwing himself under one and therefore he will. This then leads him to think: 'I *mustn't think* this way!' which leads him to think that way even more.

If you believe that thinking and feeling a certain way will cause you to physically harm somebody, you may be a person who is prone to anger and frightened of the consequences of expressing it. You may feel that you can't control it and that once you get really angry you are liable to physically assault someone as a consequence. In this case your obsessional thoughts – should they lead to physical violence to people – may be sufficiently strong to constitute a severe psychological problem requiring therapeutic intervention. But if you never get beyond thinking obsessional thoughts you might well help yourself to weaken them by vigorously disputing the irrational beliefs which create and sustain your obsessive fear of physically harming someone.

The iBs here are:
> 'I *must not* think or feel in a certain way because if I do I will harm somebody!'
> 'It's *terrible* to think that I might harm someone because of the way I think and feel!'
> 'I *can't bear* thinking and feeling this way!'

Thinking *doesn't inevitably* lead to action and if the person could learn to tolerate and accept himself with his unacceptable thoughts and feelings he would be much less likely to carry out his thoughts and feelings in action. Thus:

Dispute: Does it logically follow that because you might harm somebody when you think and feel in a certain way that therefore you mustn't think or feel in that way? If it logically followed that you absolutely must not harm somebody when you thought and felt in a certain way, then you wouldn't harm them. It would be undesirable certainly if your thinking and feeling led to somebody being harmed but there is no reason why

56

something absolutely must not happen because it would be undesirable or unfortunate.

To think that you might harm someone because of the way you think and feel is a matter of concern but it isn't terrible or awful. It isn't the worst possible thing you could imagine happening. Feeling true concern over the possibility of harming somebody will more likely help you to control yourself in the situation than becoming horribly panicked about it.

It may be unpleasant and a handicap to think and feel in a certain way but you definitely can bear it because you are bearing it. It's a disadvantage, not a holy horror.

The rational alternative to 'I can't bear thinking or feeling in a certain way because I'll harm somebody'

- 'Thinking or feeling in a certain way doesn't inevitably lead to action unless I foolishly think that it must. Since I can control how I think, I can view my tendency to irrational thinking as a problem to be overcome rather than a calamity to "awfulize" over.'
- 'It's a pain and a nuisance when I think and feel in a certain way, but that's all it is; it isn't awful or terrible.'
- 'I can certainly bear feeling and thinking a certain way although I'll never like it. Furthermore, once I can learn to accept myself as a fallible human being of value to myself and learn to *tolerate* my tendency to think and feel in a certain way, and to accept myself with it, my thinking and feeling will be much less likely to result in action because I will feel less desperate about it. Then perhaps I will start to examine why I tend to think and feel in a certain way and either replace my crazy thinking with more rational ideas, or come up with some way of adjusting more satisfactorily to my tendency to think in unacceptable ways.'

4

'I'll Do It Tomorrow . . .'

Putting off until tomorrow those things which you know would be better off being done today can turn life into one big, cluttered, unsatisfying mess! – which is a great shame. To develop your potential for more effective and enriched living, you need to examine and challenge your attitudes and maladapted behaviours because they sabotage your ability to experience life more fully and diminish your opportunities for personal growth.

In this chapter we have two objectives:

1. To show you how to identify and change faulty attitudes which encourage you to avoid doing what you really want to do, or which you avoid doing in order to 'get even' with significant others;

2. To enable you to identify and rid yourself of excuses and self-created rationalizations which encourage you to procrastinate and impede you from tackling those tasks and projects which are important to you. The key to overcoming procrastination is to ACT NOW!

What is procrastination?

Believe it or not, there are no legitimate reasons for procrastinating. There may be legitimate reasons for deferring important decisions or taking action subsequently, but there are no real *reasons* for procrastinating; only excuses and rationalizations. For example, if you have left employment and been given a lump sum of money to invest, some enterprising salesperson on hearing of your intentions may hot-foot it round to your house to persuade you to invest your money in the X–Y–Z unit trust and to do it now before the market price goes up. You may think it wiser to defer making a decision until you have had more time to think about the proposals and to compare it with alternative types of investment. That's not procrastinating, that's just common prudence. Procrastination doesn't just mean deferring taking action until more evidence is available to enable you to make an informed decision before taking the necessary action. Procrastination means *putting off* doing what your better judgement tells you can, and would better be done now.

Procrastination creates immense problems in its own right, but it can also exacerbate other existing problems you may have which then become more difficult to resolve in consequence. So, let's shed some light now on why people really procrastinate, and what they can do to rid themselves of it.

If you procrastinate – admit it!

The first thing to do if you procrastinate is to admit it. People who procrastinate tend to deny it. And there is no limit to the variety of excuses and rationalizations people resort to in order to protect their procrastinating habit. However, not everybody who procrastinates denies that they procrastinate. Some *know* they procrastinate. Moreover, they *say* they'll do something about it – someday, but somehow they never do get around to doing it! The one thing all people who procrastinate have in common – regardless of whether or not they admit their procrastination or the kind of procrastination or avoidance behaviour they practise – is a clear-cut emotional problem.

There are three main causes of avoidance behaviour and procrastination:

1. Intolerance of discomfort
2. Anxiety
3. Rebellion

Since the focus of this book is on discomfort intolerance we will devote most of this chapter to discussing under that heading the irrational beliefs and the various rationalizations and strategies stemming from these iBs which enable people to avoid doing tasks which initially involve some degree of discomfort to get them underway. This is where low frustration tolerance (LFT) comes in. Low frustration tolerance constitutes the main and most direct cause of procrastination. However, before we deal with LFT, we want to show you just briefly what lies behind two other kinds of avoidance behaviour or procrastination, termed 'ego-based' and 'rebellion-based' procrastination, respectively. The term 'ego-based' refers to a form of avoidance behaviour which is anxiety-driven, the avoidance behaviour serving to protect the person from an inferred threat to his or her self-esteem.

'Rebellion-based' procrastination is an attempt to 'get even' with some person(s) or organization for acting towards one in a manner deemed unfair or restrictive. While both of these kinds of procrastination or avoidance behaviours spring from different irrational motivations, some form of LFT can be found in almost every instance of procrastination or avoidance behaviour. Let's now look closely at the mainsprings of these three kinds of procrastination or avoidance behaviour, beginning with 'ego-based' procrastination.

Why we avoid and procrastinate

'Ego-based' procrastination We referred to this kind of procrastination as 'anxiety-driven'. Anxiety results if a person infers that the outcome to some activity in which s/he is involved may pose a threat to that person's self-esteem, and furthermore, believes that the threat must not occur, and that it would be terrible if it did. If the person also believes that s/he cannot deal effectively with the threat, or respond constructively to it should it actually occur, s/he will experience feelings of personal inadequacy. S/he then obtains short-term relief from the anxiety by withdrawing from or avoiding the inferred threat. Feelings of personal inadequacy motivate the person to avoid situations or activities which the person regards as threatening to his or her self-esteem, or sense of worth. Note that avoidance of the inferred threat enables the individual to escape the discomfort associated with anxiety in the short term but does nothing to help the person to deal constructively with the real causes of his or her anxiety. Avoidance behaviour almost always serves to perpetuate an existing problem; seldom, if ever, does it help to resolve the problem.

Anxiety and feelings of inadequacy stem from a major widely held irrational belief which goes something like this:

'I absolutely *must* perform all my important tasks adequately and win the love or approval of every person who is significant to me. If I fail, it's *awful* and therefore I am a worthless individual!'

If you believe that you *must* do well – not just prefer to do well but that you absolutely must do well at all times, there will be times when you will feel anxious at the possibility that you will fail to do as outstandingly well as you demand you must. Therefore, when you foresee a situation arising where there is a distinct possibility that you won't do outstandingly well on some task or in executing some performance, you procrastinate over doing the task, or avoid it altogether so that you can attribute your failure or lack of success, to lack of time, or to some other convenient excuse. You thereby escape the discomfort of feeling personally inadequate which you think you would have experienced had you turned out a less-than-perfect performance. If you subscribe to the irrational idea that you must do outstandingly well and be loved and approved, you won't be content to just do well; only a perfect performance will count. You must be *the* best! But because you are a fallible human you won't always succeed in turning out an outstanding performance or winning accolades from all and sundry. Sooner or later you will get a 'B' rating instead of the 'A+' you demand of yourself; the result? Down into wormhood you go! As an example of what we mean, take the case of Jenny.

Jenny enjoyed modern dancing. She had made up her mind to become the best dancer in her group so that when they all went dancing together, everyone in the group would see how well she could dance and would have to acknowledge that Jenny was 'tops'. Jenny did practise hard and learned to dance well. Soon it was acknowledged that she was the star performer of the group. Then one day, she noticed that one girl who had recently joined her group was a 'natural' – a really superb dancer. This other girl had a real flair for dancing. She was innovative and creative and could execute movements which Jenny admired and envied but which Jenny was unable to emulate with quite the style and panache this other girl possessed.

How did Jenny cope with the realization that she was no longer the best? Whenever this other girl took to the floor, Jenny always found a plausible excuse to sit that one out. When her friends beckoned her: 'C'mon, Jenny, let's go!' Jenny would say, 'No, let's have a cigarette and get a drink and just chat.' In this way, Jenny avoided direct comparison with the other girl; the group never saw Jenny and this other girl on the dance floor at the same time. After all, if you *have* to be the best at something, whether it be sports, essay-writing, dancing or whatever, and you make sure you are never seen alongside, or compared with, someone who might have a claim to be the best in your chosen field, how will anyone ever know that you are not the best as you demand that you *must* be? The demand that she *must* be the best, and the inevitable anxiety which accompanied her demand minimized Jenny's enjoyment of dancing to such an extent that she often would fail to turn up at social events where there was dancing which normally she would have loved to attend, if she thought her 'rival' was likely to be there too.

What is the answer to Jenny's dilemma? One answer would be to show her how she could dance to the best of her ability for the sheer enjoyment of it rather than for false ego-raising reasons which only perpetuate her anxiety. As we have seen, if you want to give up a self-defeating behaviour, you have to modify the irrational beliefs (iBs) which created and currently sustain it. So let's examine Jenny's iBs which are causing her to avoid or withdraw from doing what she previously had enjoyed doing.

Jenny's irrational beliefs

'I absolutely *must* be the best dancer in the group and win the approval and acknowledgement of everyone in the group. If I fail, it's *awful* and therefore I am no good!'

So long as Jenny clings to this iB, she will continue to put herself down and avoid socializing with her group whenever she perceives that she is not performing outstandingly well and rated the best dancer in the group. And even if Jenny's rival were to leave the group and enable Jenny to take over as the best dancer, Jenny's iB would still perpetuate her anxiety for she would be anxiously looking over her shoulder and wondering how long it would be before some other newcomer would appear and replace her as the best dancer. To help Jenny give up her feeling of inadequacy, she needs to identify and dispute her irrational beliefs:

'I absolutely *must* be the best dancer in the group and win the approval and acknowledgement of everyone in the group', and

'If I fail, it's *awful* and therefore I'm no good.'

Dispute: First, does it logically follow that because Jenny wants to be the best dancer and win the group's approval and acknowledgement, that she therefore *must*? Does it ever follow that because one *wants* or *desires* something that one therefore must absolutely get one's wishes fulfilled?

Second, if we believe that something we desire *must* happen, we are implying that there is some law of nature which will make it happen.

Third, what is believing that, in Jenny's case, one must be the best dancer in the group going to achieve other than anxiety and depression? Jenny might be the best dancer today, but if she absolutely insists on always being the best dancer how can she avoid being anxious over the possibility that tomorrow she may no longer be the best? Can we control the future by insisting that we *must* be the best, now and forever? No! There are no guarantees in life and if we insist on getting one, we will only store up misery for ourselves. Unless we want to live permanently on the knife-edge of anxiety, we need to give up our insistence that we must be *the* best at whatever-it-is and strive instead to do *our* best at whatever we enjoy.

Rational alternative belief (rB)

● 'I would very much prefer to be the best dancer in the group but there is no reason why I must be. Also, it would be nice to win approval from the group and acknowledgement of my ability but again there is no reason why I have to have it. Besides, the group members are entitled to their own opinions which need not agree with mine. I will more likely achieve real satisfaction and enjoyment from my dancing by dancing to the best of my ability and at the same time allowing myself to open-mindedly learn from the techniques of others I admire how to raise the standards of my own performances.'

Now, let's examine the second part of Jenny's iB

'If I fail, it's *awful* and therefore I am no good!'

Dispute: If one fails to achieve a valued goal is that really *awful*? The term 'awful' means 100 per cent bad. Now, can the fact – and just let us suppose that it is a fact, because it could be a matter of opinion – that Jenny is not the best dancer; can that fact be sensibly judged to be on a par with a major earthquake or disaster? How could we ever prove that not being voted the best dancer can be compared to the death of thousands of people? Answer: No way! It may feel great to be voted the best at some sport or activity, but just coming second or third – however disappointing personally – can hardly be called a disaster.

Next, how can not being the best dancer or the best anything, possibly destroy one's personal worth? Jenny's dancing ability is but one aspect out of literally tens of thousands of traits, characteristics, abilities and so on which go to make up Jenny. Does it really make sense to take one characteristic out of the many thousands she possesses and make that one single item a kind of barometer of her intrinsic or personal worth? Is that *all* she is – just a dancer? Again, if you think about it, the answer is: No! A single achievement or ability one possesses may be very important, but it is only *one* aspect of oneself.

Rational alternative belief (rB)

- 'It is disappointing, and possibly unfortunate, if I fail to excel and win acclaim from my peers for my performances in life, but it isn't awful or terrible. There are advantages to doing well and being highly thought of, and sometimes I can learn from others and from my own mistakes how to do even better; but my value to myself does not depend in any way upon some external validation. I can accept myself as having value to myself regardless of how well or badly I perform in sports, leisure activities or anything else in life. I do what I do because I enjoy doing it, not to gain approval or kudos from others.'

If you suffer from feelings of inadequacy, we suggest you give careful thought to these preceding paragraphs. Almost certainly you will find that the real culprit behind feelings of inadequacy and avoidance tendencies is an iB similar to Jenny's as in the case discussed above, or a variant of it. Once you identify your iB, dispute it vigorously and persistently until you see that it cannot be rationally upheld and you are able to give it up. Most importantly, learn to rate your deeds and performances, never your *self*. And give up your *'musts'*. The self-defeating philosophy, 'I *must* do perfectly well and win the approval of significant others or else it's awful and I'm no good' comes easily to many people, and our culture often fosters it. If you abandon that philosophy, we don't guarantee you'll *never* feel anxious and self-downing again, but it will certainly improve your chances of reducing or eliminating these unhelpful feelings.

Moreover, there is an additional bonus for you if you give up your anxiety-creating philosophy: it will remove one potential source of procrastination. People often procrastinate in order to protect themselves from what they regard as a painful emotional experience, such as anxiety – as you saw was the case with Jenny. If you don't feel unduly anxious, say, in attending social events you normally enjoy, you will not feel that you have to avoid them or put off participating in them. But if you feel anxious about attending social events you really would like to attend, but are afraid to risk the discomfort you predict you will feel if you do attend them, you will put off or avoid attending these events for as long as you can. You therefore remain a prisoner of your procrastination.

Rebellion-based procrastination This type of procrastination occurs when we delay doing important tasks because of our anger towards people associated with us in the performance of these tasks. Adolescents frequently anger themselves at their parents for imposing rules which they regard as over-restricting and will sullenly and resentfully try to get back at the parents by deliberately getting low grades at school or playing truant, or they may keep their room in an untidy mess, be chronically late for meals and generally uncooperative.

Adults too, can often express anger against an 'unfair' boss, for example, by behaving in a passive–aggressive manner towards the boss. Instead of expressing their resentment directly, these people procrastinate by missing deadlines, or they turn in shoddy work, waste the boss's time and try to make life as unpleasant for the boss as they can. Rebelling against doing what you know would be in your best interests to do, and which you normally would do but for your irrational demands on others, is a form of avoidance or procrastination which sooner or later will prove self-defeating. Angelo was a case in point:

Angelo supervised a team of salesmen whose job it was to supply clients with wallpaper and paints produced by the company Angelo worked for. Each month, Angelo collected his sales team's reports and submitted them to his boss who was the department head. One day the boss told Angelo that from now on, he, Angelo had to prepare summaries of all his sales team's reports to save the boss from ploughing through each salesman's report individually. 'I just cannot spare the time to examine each man's report for myself', said Angelo's boss, 'I want a summary prepared so that I can fairly quickly ascertain how the department is making out and what action I may need to take to meet our business targets. I shall want your summary ready for me to see by 9.00 am on the first working day of each month.' Angelo just said: 'OK', but inwardly he was seething.

'He has no right to give me all this extra work! It will be difficult and it *shouldn't* be so difficult! I've got enough on my plate trying to organize the rounds of my sales team without having him wanting blasted summaries of their activities each month! I'll show him!' was Angelo's response; 'He's made up his mind to stick this on me; he *mustn't* treat me like this! He's a sadist for treating me like this.' While Angelo fumed over his 'unfair' treatment he told himself, 'I won't stand for it! I can sabotage his goals, I'll refuse to do what he wants, I won't let him make me suffer. I'll do the minimum of work, he'll get his damned summaries but they'll be late and if I alter a figure here and there to make things look bleaker than they really are already, how's he to know? Now, that's a thought! He might then get a bollicking from his own boss for our poor results and that would really fix his wagon! That'll teach him! That'll prove I can't be kicked around!'

After a few months during which Angelo rebelliously procrastinated over getting his work out in time in order to 'prove I'm not going to be pushed around', the outcome was that Angelo – not his boss – was demoted. Because of his hostile rebelliousness Angelo lost control of himself and subsequently his job in his self-defeating 'ego' battle with his boss.

How could Angelo more rationally have behaved in this situation?

First, he could have questioned his attributions and assumptions: (a) 'Is it really true that my boss has no right to give me extra work? Isn't that what he's there for, to allocate work as he sees fit?'; (b) 'Where's the evidence that my boss has sadistic feelings towards me and wants to do me down? True, he gave me extra work, but isn't there a good reason for it? Isn't it just conceivable that studying a properly prepared summary of the sales team's activities each month would be a more efficient use of a department head's time than studying each salesman's report individually? And wouldn't the reports only make sense then by being summarized anyway?'

Next, Angelo would be encouraged to ferret out and dispute his iBs about being given the extra work and to come up with rational alternative beliefs (rBs).

The irrational beliefs

'It will be difficult and it *shouldn't* be so difficult!'

Dispute: Granted that the extra work is a nuisance and may be difficult to get out in time, but why shouldn't it be difficult? If a task is difficult, it's difficult. There is no reason why it shouldn't be difficult if it is; nor is there any reason why you shouldn't be given the extra work. You are presumably being paid to do it!

Rational alternative belief (rB)

- 'Since I am employed in a supervisory capacity there is no reason why I should not have been given this extra work which after all is part of my job. I would prefer this extra work of preparing summaries to be easy rather than difficult but there is no reason why it has to be easy. If it's difficult, it's difficult. Maybe if I stop moaning about the difficulty and get on with it, I will find it getting easier the more frequently I do it.'

'He *mustn't* treat me like this!'
'He's a sadist for treating me like this!'

Dispute: Even if your boss is picking you out specially and treating you badly, what law says he *mustn't* treat you badly? If there was such a law, he would have no choice but to treat you well. Obviously there is no such law! Moreover, is giving you extra work proof that he is treating you badly, let alone sadistically? Many people do extra work from time to time. Is that proof of ill treatment? Most unlikely! Extra work is extra work. Even if you could prove you'd been treated unreasonably, you don't have to stay in the job and could always leave it.

Rational alternative belief (rB)

- 'Although I would prefer my boss to treat me the way I want to be treated there is no reason why he has to. As the boss, he can please himself, within reason, as to how he treats his staff. I may not be enthusiastic about him giving me that extra work but that hardly makes him a sadist. Maybe I'll never like working for this guy, but so long as I choose to stay and work for him I can stand it. So I would be wise to accept the reality of the situation and stop giving myself needless pain over the way my boss chooses to run his business.'

The point being made here is that while lots of things, events or people may contribute to your hostile feelings, you yourself create your angry feelings. If you devoutly believe that *they* – things, events and people outside – *make* you angry, you evade admitting your *own* responsibility for your feelings. From there it is only a step to the point where your resentment allies itself with procrastination to bring on all those self-defeating results you can do without. Once you determine not to upset yourself over the unfairnesses and other hassles the world puts in your way, your resentment and over-rebelliousness will diminish to the point where you can adequately cope with, rather than over-react to, these unpleasant events.

Low frustration tolerance (LFT) In Chapter 1 we showed how LFT keeps us in the Comfort Trap. We outlined the difference between short-range and long-range hedonism, and argued that LFT springs from short-range hedonism. Short-range hedonism, you may recall, is the philosophy that one must be comfortable in the moment: not just occasionally, but practically all the time; only the present counts; the future can take care of itself; therefore one should go for instant gratification and not concern oneself too much about the possibility that pleasure now may mean less pleasure, or even pain, later. Long-range hedonism, by contrast, takes a saner view: being comfortable now is fine provided that in going for immediate gains or pleasures you don't sacrifice greater gains or pleasures in the longer term. Long-range hedonism also advocates putting up with present pains for the sake of future gains. As Benjamin Franklin wisely noted: 'There are no gains without pains!'

Low frustration tolerance arises when we quite rightly recognize that in order to obtain some *future* gain we have to undergo some degree of *present* pain, but see that present pain as *too* painful, *too* uncomfortable and *too* much to put up with even if we realize we would obtain future gains or advantages by putting up with the short-term discomfort.

The philosophy at the core of LFT can be stated as: 'I cannot stand present pain for future gain'. This, in turn, derives from a major irrational belief which says: 'Because it is desirable that I experience pleasure rather than pain, the world absolutely should arrange this and life is horrible, and I can't bear it when the world doesn't'.

When people are unwilling to admit, even to themselves, that they can't stand present pain for future gain, they come out with plausible excuses or rationalizations to justify their inactivity and procrastination in the face of unpleasant or difficult tasks they know darned well ought to be done promptly to avoid greater difficulties and complications later.

The kind of rationalizations people come out with to justify their procrastinating are often related to whether the contemplated task is seen as relatively easy or complex.

Simple tasks: rationalisations used to justify procrastination

'I'll do it when I feel in the mood'
'I don't feel like doing it now!'
'I'll do it tomorrow!'

Anna decided to celebrate her 21st birthday by having a party in her flat. With a little help from friends, Anna provided a large buffet and added a generous amount of wine, beers and spirits at her own expense. Some 40 invited friends and colleagues from work turned up on the day and a great time was had by all. When the last guest had left, Anna looked around her apartment. Dirty dishes were everywhere! There were piles of empty bottles, and beer cans covered every square inch of working surface in the kitchen, to say nothing of the floor! There were empty and half-empty glasses standing or lying on any conveniently available place throughout the apartment, including the carpet! A few glasses were broken. Surveying the mess, Anna thought: 'I can't face cleaning up now, it's 5 am, I'll get some sleep and clean up in the morning!'

It was nearly 2 pm before Anna woke. She had a bit of a hangover. She decided to wait till the evening when her hangover would probably have gone and then she would tackle the cleaning up. By 8 o'clock that evening Anna's hangover had gone, but when she looked at the mountain of work awaiting her attention, Anna shuddered and decided to leave the clearing and cleaning up for another day, telling herself: 'I don't feel like it, I'll do it tomorrow!' By leaving it another day, Anna realized that she would miss the refuse collection due to be called for early the following morning and that this would mean having to retain several sacks of rubbish in her flat until the following week. Cursing the refuse collectors for not calling at more 'convenient' times, Anna settled down to watch a movie on TV. Anna told herself: 'I'll do the cleaning up tomorrow when I feel in the mood.' The next day, Anna had a busy day in the office and felt too tired on returning home to make a start on cleaning up her apartment which by now was looking even worse as a result of unwashed dishes Anna had accumulated from her own meals following the party. 'What a tip!', thought Anna in disgust, 'Why should I have to do all this clearing up?' In desperation, Anna phoned for a cleaning firm to come over in the morning and clean up for her, even though she knew she could not afford the additional expense of hiring labour in addition to the outlay she had incurred in preparing for the party.

The consequence of her procrastination was that Anna ended up paying a higher price than she had intended for her 21st birthday celebration, and she felt ashamed of herself for having allowed it all to get on top of her.

Anna's procrastination stemmed from her low tolerance of discomfort. 'I have to be comfortable in the moment!' was her basic philosophy. Since cleaning up after her party involved some discomfort, Anna readily convinced herself to postpone the task until she felt like it. She would do it when she felt in the mood. Many people share Anna's belief that it is better to wait until they feel in the mood before tackling some task which may involve a degree of effort or discomfort.

Why is this rationalization self-defeating and therefore likely to make things worse, rather than better?

1. It may be possible that a time will come when you feel in the mood to carry out some task and that you will then find it easier to do. But there's no guarantee! That hoped-for time may never come, and even if it does, you may wait a long time for it.

2. That time when you feel in the mood to accomplish your task may arrive so late as to cause public concern. For example, if Anna delayed cleaning up her apartment until she felt in the mood – which might mean waiting for several days – or even weeks, she might find herself with a potential, or actual health problem on her hands!

3. Even if you do manage to get in the right mood within a reasonable period of time, and get your task done, the advantage of doing so may be outweighed by the disadvantages arising from the accumulation of other jobs which has come about because of your procrastination on this one. Doing your present task promptly enables you to schedule adequate time for carrying out these other jobs awaiting your attention.

Merely becoming aware of the self-defeating consequences of your rationalizations for procrastinating isn't by itself likely to help you to give them up. To give up any unhelpful habit that has become established requires a fundamental change in one's attitude towards it. Presently we will describe a number of different techniques aimed at helping people to achieve just such a fundamental change in their basic procrastination-creating philosophies. For the moment, let's look at several other excuses and stratagems people commonly adopt to avoid the discomfort of tackling projects which call for immediate or early attention.

Involving oneself in 'pseudo-work'

This is another way of refusing to acknowledge that you have a real problem with procrastination. You are not prepared to make yourself uncomfortable in the short term in order to gain long-term advantages. So you hide this unpalatable fact from yourself by busying yourself in some other activity which you find easier or more interesting. Since you cannot do two things at once, you conveniently avoid tackling the more urgent but less pleasant task awaiting your early attention and delude yourself that you are not really procrastinating at all! You may even convince yourself that the pseudo-task you throw yourself into with self-righteous enthusiasm is more important, or even more essential, than your main task.

> Robert had a project to write up and send to his tutor by a specified date; already he was running late. Robert hated writing up the results of his experiments and needed little excuse to find some distraction he found more comfortable or interesting. Thus, when Robert realized that time was passing and that it would be better to get cracking on writing up his project, he would decide his study room needed tidying up. How could he possibly be expected to work in such an untidy environment? Robert would then rearrange his papers, or he would shift his books around in the bookcase to put them in a more 'logical' order. Or he would see if he had any outstanding bills to pay and proceed to occupy himself in writing cheques to those he owed money to. 'I can't stand writing up my project notes with all this clutter around!' he told himself, as yet more valuable time was spent in activities of secondary importance while his more urgent project was further delayed.

Once more we have an example of the iB: 'I can't stand present pain for future gain!' Do either of the examples of procrastination we've just discussed ring a bell with you? Many people react in the same way as Anna and Robert do when faced with the unpalatable or difficult tasks they know should be done now in order to avoid having to deal with bigger problems later.

Let's see what methods we could use to bypass the kind of rationalizations discussed in this section and help people become effectively task-oriented. Then we shall go on to deal with the rationalizations people trick themselves with when facing more complex or difficult tasks.

Combating procrastination

Cognitive methods

Inappropriate feelings and behaviours, such as elaborately avoiding tackling those tasks which are important to you, stem from faulty ways of thinking. In other words, if you hold irrational beliefs about yourself and the world, these beliefs will lead to disturbed feelings and self-defeating behaviours. Take the cases of Anna and Robert: both of them have a low tolerance of discomfort. Their circumstances are different but they hold the same irrational belief about their circumstances, viz:

The irrational beliefs

'If certain things are undesirable, but unavoidable if I am to get what I want, then these things ought not to exist, and I can't stand it if they do!'

Doesn't it sound familiar? In fact, that iB is a close relative of major irrational belief: 'Because it is preferable that I experience pleasure rather than pain, the world absolutely should arrange this, and life is horrible, and I can't bear it when the world does not.'

Let's dispute the iB held by Anna and Robert to see if their belief accords with reality.

Dispute: If you view some task as undesirable but see it as necessary to achieve some goal or objective, in what way can you logically believe that it should not exist? Isn't it a logical contradiction to claim that something is necessary but that it should not exist? If it exists it necessarily exists because it does exist.

Is there a law of the universe which says that you must not experience unpleasant or undesirable things? Is there a law which names you as some kind of special person who *deserves* to have life made easy and enjoyable for you and for whom inconveniences and hassles *must not* exist? If there were such a law you obviously would not be demanding that undesirable things should not exist because they couldn't exist!

As for your claim: 'If undesirable things exist [as they *shouldn't*], I can't stand it', you can't be serious! You haven't died yet because undesirable things exist, which you would have done if you really could not stand them. The fact is that you can stand anything until the moment you die. After that, you won't care!

What rational alternative beliefs could you suggest to replace these very irrational beliefs of Anna and Robert?

Rational alternative belief (rB)

- 'If certain things are undesirable but at the same time cannot be avoided if I am to achieve my goals and objectives, then it's tough! In the pursuit of my goals I would certainly prefer that certain things could be avoided but there is no reason why the world must be as I would like it to be. Nor is there any reason why things that are undesirable should not exist. What exists, exists! I can obviously stand conditions whether I like them or not, and so long as I plan and strive for what I want I would be wise to accept that I can stand present inconvenience and discomfort in order to gain the advantages I seek.'

Whining about the hassles you have to overcome to reach your objectives in life will promote your procrastinating tendencies; pushing yourself to *act* against these tendencies, stops them.

Emotive methods

Our theory of human emotions and behaviour states that how we think largely determines how we feel and behave. Not completely, of course, because drugs and physiological states can act on the brain directly and influence our perceptions and interpretations of what is going on. But under the usual conditions in which you lead your life, a lightly held belief about something will generally lead to a mild feeling about it. For example, if you believe: 'I don't find much pleasure in doing all the washing and clearing up after a party', you will tend to feel a mild dislike for actually doing the washing and clearing up. And if you believe: 'I find writing up my experimental project less exciting than carrying out the actual experiments', you will feel somewhat unenthusiastic about actually doing the writing up, but you will still do it.

However, if you are like Anna and believe, 'I *loathe* washing and clearing up after a party! I feel sick just thinking about it!', these much stronger feelings will tend to block you from tackling the washing up. Similarly, if you go along with Robert's belief: 'I *hate* writing up my experimental projects! It shouldn't involve so much work!', you will feel very unwilling to face the discomfort and get down to writing up your project and you will look for excuses to enable you to avoid doing it.

If you strongly hold negative irrational beliefs about some activity or project, you will normally tend to have strong negative feelings about undertaking the activity or project. So, what's the answer to changing these unhelpful ideas and feelings which block you from engaging in the disliked activities? Answer: *vigorously* and *forcefully* attack the foolish ideas – especially your 'musts' and absolute 'shoulds' which lie behind your negative attitudes. For example, if you believe: 'Clearing up after a big party means *too* much work to do! It *shouldn't* be so much! How unfair that I have to do it!', you can vigorously counter-attack such statements with:

- 'Nothing amounts to *too* much work! It's only much work! If 40 people attend a party with buffet and drinks provided, there *must* be an enormous amount of clearing up to do afterwards because there *is*! No matter how much of a hassle it is, I definitely *can* do it! And I darned well *will* do it so that I can get back to my normal daily living routines as soon as possible!'

Again, if you are finding difficulty in getting down to that writing project and are telling yourself: 'It *shouldn't* involve so much work! I don't find writing easy! It's really *too* hard!', you can combat these silly ideas by vigorously and forcefully drumming into your head, until you truly believe them, counter-attacking ideas such as these:

- 'Writing up my project *should* involve much work, because it *does*! So I don't find writing easy! Where is the law that says writing *must* be easy? And if writing is hard, it's hard! Nothing is *too* hard – only *hard*! I definitely can write up my project and I'd better, unless I want to waste a whole term's work!'

Practise these self-statements forcefully and frequently until you truly come to believe them. If you merely repeat them to yourself in a namby-pamby manner they won't really sink in and therefore will do you little good. By forcefully and persistently repeating these rational self-statements you can more effectively persuade yourself that you don't *have* to procrastinate and that you *can* stand doing uncomfortable or onerous tasks.

Behavioural methods

If you add some action techniques to the thinking and emotive methods you have already studied, you will bring even more 'firepower' to the task of reducing or eliminating your procrastination. We are indebted to a colleague of ours, Michael E Bernard PhD, Fellow and Co-Director of the Australian Institute for Rational-Emotive Therapy for the following suggestions:

The bits and pieces approach

This technique consists in breaking down the task facing you into bits and pieces, which are not overwhelming in themselves and which can be more easily tackled. By doing even one bit of the total task, the rest of the task becomes automatically less intimidating. Take, for example, Anna's problem when she faced that mountain of dishes, plates and glasses etc. following her party. Before retiring to bed, Anna could collect all the glasses and immerse them in a large basin of soapy water while she collected up, say, all the empty beer cans and bottles and put them in plastic refuse sacks. That would eliminate two parts of the total job. Next day she could finish washing and drying the glasses and start on the plates and dishes. In short, this technique helps you to break the inertia and get going. By focusing on one job at a time, you get yourself started and then the rest of the task doesn't seem so overwhelming.

The five-minute plan

This is a good way of getting started on an activity which is going to take a bit of time. If you are like Robert and find difficulty in getting started on a writing project, such as writing a chapter for a book or preparing a thesis, writing up the details of an experiment you have carried out, or devising a strategic business plan for your organization, the key is to make a start. In the five-minute plan, you make an agreement with yourself to start on your project and stay with it for at least five minutes. At the end of five minutes you review the situation and ask yourself whether you wish to continue for another five minutes. You don't *have* to continue beyond the original time period but you allow your actions to serve as your answer. If you are like most people you will find that the inertia begins to take hold by the end of the first five minutes and you feel more comfortable remaining where you are. So you contract with yourself to do another five minutes – and another! Getting into gear at the start is the hardest part. But once you are in gear you tend to find it easier to remain in gear. In other words, you use the principle of inertia to help you *do* – not stew!

This technique as well as the preceding one can also be used appropriately to tackle the 'party' problem that faced Anna. We suggest you try each of them the next time you find yourself procrastinating over the kind of problem which beset Anna and Robert. We think these problems are typical of the lifestyles of many people living in today's world. In fact, we ourselves have personally encountered both of the problem scenarios experienced by Anna and Robert – and on more than one occasion, so we know what we are talking about!

Complex tasks: rationalizations used to justify procrastination

Here we look at the rationalizations people offer for not tackling tasks which are complex and usually more difficult than the relatively simple tasks discussed in the previous sections.

Typically a person will look at a task, realize that it is complex and convince him-/herself: 'It's *too* hard! It *shouldn't* be as difficult as it is!' Telling yourself this only makes the task harder than it otherwise would be.

Two mountaineers were confronted with a very tough mountain not far off the scale of Everest. The first mountaineer studied the mountain and declared: 'It's going to be difficult, but not *too* difficult.' The second mountaineer studied the mountain and concluded: 'It's big, and it's *too* hard!'

The first man began to draw up a plan of ascent. His belief that the ascent would be difficult, but not too difficult and therefore possible, motivated him to start preparing a feasible plan to climb the mountain. This man believed: 'It's difficult, but it should be as difficult as it is.'

The second man however, saw no point in preparing a plan. His belief that climbing the mountain would not only be hard, but *too* hard undermined his resolve and stopped him from making any plans to climb that mountain. By exaggerating the difficulty in climbing the mountain, the second man blew up the task, made it look more difficult than it was, and thus stopped himself from doing anything practical to solve the problem.

'I have to feel comfortable doing it'

There's no law of the universe which says that you *have* to feel comfortable before approaching a complex task. In fact you are unlikely to feel comfortable when taking on a complex task because such tasks are not usually designed with comfort in mind. You may become comfortable later as you gain experience in doing the task but you are unlikely to feel comfortable when you *first* encounter it. You could dispute your belief that you have to be comfortable by asking yourself: 'What is so intolerable about experiencing discomfort when tackling an unfamiliar task?' Answer: 'I make it intolerable by defining it as "awful" and telling myself that it's unbearable!' Unless you give up the nutty notion that you have to be comfortable before you start a complex task, the chances are you'll never start it.

'I have to be certain before I begin that it'll turn out right'

If you have to be certain of your task or project turning out right before you begin it, aren't you demanding a guarantee of success? Well, good luck! Who is going to write you that guarantee? All life carries an element of risk, and, like it or not, we would be wise to recognize and accept this. 'What! No guarantees!' Right! There are no guarantees. 'But what if I meet with instant success? Doesn't that mean that I can be certain that it will all turn out right in the end?' Answer: not necessarily. Maybe you will be an *instant* success – with that new partner you've fallen for, or with that new song you've written for the charts, but that is only the beginning. You cannot be certain that you'll continue to be successful until you actually finish your task successfully. Then, and only then, will you feel certain about the outcome because you *have* achieved it. Someone once remarked that it is one thing to create a reputation; it's quite another thing to maintain it! If you are sitting debating with yourself: 'Can I be certain this will turn out right?' your best bet is to try it and see. If you really work at it – and we mean w-o-r-k – you will stand a much better chance of achieving a successful outcome than if you merely sit and whine for a guarantee.

'I have to be confident that I can do it!'

So you have to feel confident you can carry out your task! This is similar to the rationalization above; both are classic examples of putting the cart before the horse. How can you become confident of doing anything you haven't tried before until you actually do it? Let's say you have begun a course in public speaking. Your goal is to be able to speak fluently and confidently in public on subjects which are your special concern. A good teacher will teach you the elements of public speaking, what to do, and what not to do. But merely knowing what to do won't make you a public speaker any more than knowing what to do when you are in the driving seat of an automobile will make you a driver. Knowing 'what' is important, but not until you actually 'do' can you claim to know 'how'.

Thus, forcing yourself to speak in public *un*confidently constitutes the best way of learning to speak confidently. You will learn from your mistakes and the more often you take the opportunity to speak in public the sooner will you reach the stage where you can speak confidently. Until you actually get up and *speak*, all the self-talk in the world – 'I know I can do it, I know I can do it!' – will not convince you thoroughly until you actually *do* get up and speak. 'I know I can', merely means you *think* you can; whereas, when you actually speak in public, you have evidence that you really *can*. In short, confidence comes with doing. There is simply no other way to acquire it.

'*I have to feel I am in control of it!*'

If your demand to be in control before you launch yourself into performing some task or project means that you must be able to control environmental contingencies to coincide with your personal wishes, you are really on a hiding to nothing. For how can you control all possible environmental contingencies that might affect the outcome of your project? Even if you do feel in control at some point in your project, you will tend to worry over how long you'll continue to feel in control and how awful it would be if you lost control. In reality, you may have some partial control over external circumstances, but your best bet is to learn how to control yourself. None of us has total or complete control over ourselves, of course, but we do have some, and more than most people realize. You can largely control how you think and feel because you have the power of choice. If you decide to use that power to direct your life in accordance with your wishes and goals, rather than try to control the world around you, you will more likely achieve more of what you want and less of what you don't want.

To summarize, if you allow yourself to avoid tackling complex or difficult tasks until you feel comfortable, or confident, or certain of success, or always in control of external contingencies, you may wait for ever. If you push yourself into doing things uncomfortably, with uncertainty, unconfidently and when you don't feel in control of events, you will definitely undermine your procrastinating tendencies and begin to *do* – rather than stew.

Other avoidances

'I need the anxiety to do it!'

This means delaying starting a task or project until the last minute. The pressure of time builds up, you become anxious over the fear of not doing the job by the target date or of being criticized for being late. This fear then galvanizes you into action! But now you also have a great excuse for being late, or for not doing the job properly, for you can now claim: 'If only I had started earlier I could have completed the job on time!' or 'If I'd been able to start earlier, I could have done a much better job!'

Waiting until the last minute when you begin to panic about getting the job done in time – or even getting it done at all – may be one way of tackling a time-limited job, but is it really necessary to 'put your neck under the guillotine' like that? Isn't the job harder to do under those conditions? Is the job as well done as it might be if you gave yourself more time to assemble all the relevant material, to explore alternative ways of doing it and to check and re-check your finished product for errors, or sloppy work or evidence of having done a rushed job rather than your best job? Consider: it isn't the pressure that 'makes' you finish the task by the due date. *You* finish the task because when you feel the pressure you tell yourself: 'Now I really *have* to get cracking and finish this task!' You define the conditions under which you do the job as necessitating last minute pressure. But you could, alternatively, tell yourself, long before the pressure mounts up: 'I'd better make a start now and get the good results I want without having to cram it all in to the last few days and hours. So far I've managed to get fairly good results, but I could get even better results if I took my time. Besides, I don't like the tension and pain I bring on myself by rushing the job. I have to give up certain pleasures and I even lose sleep. So is it worth it? Maybe I would be wise to pace myself next time a similar job comes up, start on it in good time and get the results I want without the hassle and pain I get through procrastinating until the last minute.' Why don't you try doing the job *unanxiously* the next time? You have nothing to lose, only the pain and tension that goes with doing the job *with* anxiety.

Getting somebody else to do it

A subtle form of avoidance practised by some people is to manipulate other people or the environment in such a way as to encourage those others to do tasks proper to the person practising the avoidance.

Wheedling is used, or praise may be given in the form: 'I know you are much better at doing this job than I am!' In an office, a person may absent him- or herself at a strategic moment, and even for a considerable period of time, in order to avoid some unliked task in the knowledge that someone else will then be asked to pick up the job and do it.

The object of these manoeuvres is to enable someone to avoid the discomfort of doing some onerous job or task for which they have the responsibility, by encouraging somebody else to do it instead. These people avoid their own discomfort and they feel OK in the short term, but they reap the following disadvantages:

- they don't confront their fear
- they don't learn the skills they would learn if they did confront their fears. As a result, they end up by experiencing *chronic* discomfort rather than the acute, but shorter duration discomfort they would experience if they did confront their fear.

If you have still to find this out by experiencing it, we would like to assure you that once you get into a task, you will see that it isn't as uncomfortable or as difficult as you thought it would be, and if you stick with it, you'll often achieve a good deal more than if you waited until inspiration came, or until you felt more comfortable. If you wait until you feel comfortable, or 'in the mood', you can wait a long time.

In general, do whatever task you have set yourself, earlier rather than later; otherwise you tend to practise and reinforce your irrational beliefs and rationalizations such as: 'It's *too* hard, and it *shouldn't* be so hard'; 'I have to be comfortable'; 'I have to be confident', and so on. Realize too, that the more you procrastinate the more likely it is that unforeseen circumstances will arise to interfere with your doing something. You can think of procrastination as pointless self-penalization: you deliberately penalize yourself but gain nothing by doing so.

More techniques to combat procrastination

Referenting

This technique is designed to get you motivated to stop procrastinating and make a start on some important project. Let's assume you want to embark on a fitness programme you can carry out at home but you keep procrastinating on starting it. You've read books on exercise and you know what you need to do but still you hold back on getting started.

What you do is to make a list of all the good things which will happen if you stop procrastinating and of all the miserable results you'll get by continuing to procrastinate. Michael Bernard writes:

It's very human to think about the disadvantages of doing something immediately (frustration, discomfort) and the advantages of delaying (immediate pleasure, absence of misery). This tendency makes it especially hard for you to break long-standing bad habits as it destroys any motivation you will need to get going.

Referenting helps you to put a break on your short-term hedonistic impulses and to begin to enjoy the advantages of gaining control over your self-defeating habits and the long-term benefits which accrue from it.

Forcing yourself to, say, exercise regularly provides you with evidence that you definitely *can* do it. Establish an exercise routine; set aside a time and place to practise your exercises on a daily basis. At first, it may seem strange and uncomfortable but if you persist until exercising becomes a habit, you will find it easier, more comfortable and even enjoyable. Reminding yourself from time to time of the advantages you'll derive from exercising as well as the disadvantages from not exercising will help to keep your motivation high.

Establish priorities

Once you stop procrastinating you may find yourself enthusiastically committed to accomplishing so many tasks each day that you find there is literally not enough time to do everything. It is important to have a clear idea of which are the most important things to get done and which are the less important. Knowing the most important ones, you can concentrate on getting these done, so that if you run out of time you delay or procrastinate on the less important things. You can use files or other review methods to enable you to keep track of where you stand each day so that you use your time in the most efficient way to accomplish your priority-graded tasks.

Make a reminder file

This can be a large appointment book or desk calendar where each page denotes one day. Suppose you have bills to pay and other time-limited items to attend to such as phone bills, utility bills, your tax return, an anniversary card, and so on. You establish the dates when these items are due to be paid or sent out, and then you insert the bill or tax form or personal reminder into your appointment book on the appropriate page. Comes the day when a bill or tax form is due, you deal with it right there and then. If you delay and miss the deadline for posting, you put the delayed item back into the book on the following day's page where it will join those items already awaiting your attention on that day. You do this every single day you procrastinate until you fill out that tax return or pay that delayed electricity bill. The sight of your untidy looking appointment book cluttered with unpaid bills, etc, can stimulate your resolve to deal with these matters by their due dates, or even earlier.

Self-management strategies

When you find it difficult to get going on a task you have set yourself to do at a set time, you can adopt the self-management techniques we described in some detail in Chapter 1. To recap briefly, these techniques enable you to, literally, reinforce yourself with some satisfier that you personally enjoy soon after you have carried out your task instead of procrastinating over it. But if you procrastinate you not only do without your 'reward' but you can also penalize yourself with something you abhor immediately after you procrastinate. If you force yourself to really carry out these reinforcements and penalties you can undermine your procrastinating tendencies and significantly reduce or overcome them.

Do you feel you are in a rut?

If you feel you are in some kind of a rut and want to get out of it, the anti-procrastination techniques we have been discussing should prove helpful.

Being in a rut is very similar to being in the Comfort Trap, which is why the methods you have been learning to beat the Comfort Trap will come in useful once you really make a determined effort to break out of your prison. For that is what being in a rut feels like: You feel unhappy, hemmed in, frustrated, bored; you want out, but you don't quite know how; and at the same time you feel a bit uneasy about change, and about what lies ahead for you if you do break out of familiar surroundings into unfamiliar ones. You may not like your rut, but you have become accustomed to it. You have become set in a pattern of familiar but bearable chronic discomfort. The thought of change and the uncertainty and possible pain that might go with change sets your alarm bells ringing.

We will presently outline a strategy for breaking out of ruts. But first, let's make clear what a rut is, and how to tell if you are in one. We shall also mention the main kinds of ruts people get into. Nearly everyone has been in a rut at some time or other. So, don't think you are alone.

Typical features of a rut

The following features typify a rut:

1. A sense of being stuck, of getting nowhere
2. A pervasive sense of boredom, of monotony
3. Self-doubts, a lowered sense of self-worth

4. Repetition of unsatisfying or pointless routines
5. Fear of change
6. A strong desire to avoid discomfort
7. Being resigned to the situation
8. A feeling of hopelessness and helplessness bordering on depression.

Now, draw up a self-questionnaire and answer each of these 8 items by writing down opposite each item one of the following words: rarely; occasionally; frequently; or always. Score 1 for rarely, score 2 for occasionally and score 3 for frequently or always. Then add up your score. A score of 8–13 means you see yourself as having a fairly mild problem. If your score lies between 14 and 20 it's looking serious. If you are between 21 and 24 it means you see yourself as having a very serious rut problem.

Although ruts are characterized by routine-like habit patterns, not all routine behaviours can be classed as ruts. Many of our daily routines are pleasant to perform and represent an efficient use of time. They provide a structure around which we organize our lives. Some people, too, really prefer a stable, predictable, highly structured pattern to their lives and are content and happy to live that way.

Ruts, on the other hand, are like energy-sapping black holes. People in ruts are people in quandaries; they are unhappy with their situation but fear the consequences of making any radical changes. Or perhaps they did try to change, and failed to make it. Now they see no hope of successfully changing their life and are resigned to the situation.

Three main kinds of rut

As William J Knaus points out in *How To Get Out Of A Rut* (1982), there are three kinds of rut: career, interpersonal, and recreational.

Career rut

'Career' covers your work or vocation. If you are unhappy in your work, feel that you are just spinning your wheels but are doing nothing to change that unsatisfying pattern, you are in a career rut.

Interpersonal rut

Is your relationship with some particular person continually strained or boring and you are doing nothing to change the pattern? Or are you in a destructive, dead-end marriage or relationship and are doing nothing to end it? If you can answer 'Yes' to either of these questions, you are in an interpersonal rut.

Recreational rut

This refers to your leisure-time activities. For example, do you still go round to the club you've been going to for years, see the same old faces, talk about the same old things and feel thoroughly bored but can think of nothing different to occupy yourself and are doing nothing about it? If so, you are in a recreational rut.

Why you remain in a rut

Let's assume you have identified some aspect of your life as being in a rut. You have achieved a score on the 8-item test which convinces you that the problem is sufficiently serious to merit action to get out of your rut. Your next step is to determine accurately why you are in your present rut. Unless you clearly define the problem, you are unlikely to arrive at the most effective way of resolving it.

There are two possibilities to consider:

If your problem is self-created

This means that you could break free from your rut but are failing to do so because you are locked into a pattern of negative thinking and irrational beliefs.

If your problem refers to circumstances beyond your immediate control

You may not be in a rut, technically speaking, but you may be using these circumstances as an excuse for getting into a rut and staying in it. Nevertheless, certain external circumstances can inhibit you from acting as you would wish. For example, you may be in a dead-end job with no prospect of advancement, but are tied to it because you have a heavy debt or mortgage to pay off. Or you may be handicapped in some way whereby your freedom of decision or freedom of movement is restricted. Honestly facing up to such problems may feel uncomfortable, at least temporarily, but confronting problems will tend to get you ahead faster than avoiding them. Such situational problems may seem daunting but few, if any, are completely hopeless.

Once a problem of external circumstances has been overcome, or reduced to manageable proportions, you are then in a position to look for any negative attitudes, self-created fears or rationalizations which may be pushing you into a rut or keeping you in one.

What it takes to break free

First, you need a commitment to change. If you are still resisting breaking an unwanted pattern in your life, if you are still putting up with boring, monotonous, unfulfilling routines, then either your commitment is only half-hearted, or you are resisting taking constructive action to break free of your rut because:

1. You have accustomed yourself to living with a bearable level of chronic discomfort through being familiar with it.
2. You are avoiding the short-term but more acute discomfort implicit in making a fundamental change.
3. You cling to a number of other unrealistic notions and irrational beliefs which muddy and distort your view of reality.

In previous sections we pointed out that low frustration tolerance (LFT) is the most frequent cause of procrastination. Avoidance of discomfort is characteristic of LFT and the irrational belief that life must be easy and grant one what one wants without too much effort or pain, is central to LFT. Can you see that LFT is the driving force behind the first two reasons listed above? 'I have to be comfortable!' Does that ring a bell? You now have experience in disputing the notion: 'I have to be comfortable in the moment', or 'I can't bear discomfort in the short term even when it would be in my long-term interests to bear it'. If you need to refresh your memory, return to the sections on LFT which appear earlier in this chapter.

What other iBs under the third reason above could be holding you back from acting now to break your rut pattern? How about checking the items on the 8-point list of typical features of a rut? How about fear of change? What is it you're really afraid of? Are you afraid you can't cope with say, a move to a new and better job? If so, where is the evidence that you can't cope? Or, are you afraid of what people will think of you if you leave a bad relationship? Or perhaps you have self-doubts: perhaps you doubt your ability to change and are damning yourself for having wasted so many years already in a rut of your own making that you feel no good and are certain you have left it too late to do anything about it now?

All of these fears – regardless of how they are expressed – stem from negative, distorted or exaggerated thinking. As with all the other irrational beliefs you have met in this, and in previous chapters, take each belief and challenge it; question it; is there any real evidence to support it? People procrastinate largely because they think they have to be comfortable in the moment. Consequently, they tend to exaggerate the allegedly fearful things that could happen to them if something disturbs the normal pattern of their lives. Dispute your fears. Convince yourself that while real dangers exist in the world and can strike at any time and in any place, mental fear is manufactured. It's a self-created fear which exists only in your head! It may have contributed to your miseries in the past but it has no power to blight your future unless you insist on taking it with you. Dump it! And study those thinking and acting methods we suggested you use to combat procrastination, perfectionism and self-depreciation, and use them to conquer any life-depleting ruts which are currently holding you back from enjoying a more productive and fulfilling life.

Concluding remarks

When we try to erect defences against honestly facing up to, and acknowledging, our procrastination, we resort to various self-deceptions and rationalizations. These rationalizations or excuses may *sound* reasonable because they are in effect promises we make to ourselves to do some task at a more 'convenient' future time. By postponing the task to some time in the future – usually unspecified(!), we don't have to worry about doing it today. We really intend to do it later! Unfortunately we may delay doing the task for so long that it is no longer worth doing or it has ceased to be relevant. If you feel tempted to use this as an excuse to delay doing some task indefinitely, resist the temptation! The idea that by delaying something indefinitely so that it does not matter anymore may sound attractive to some and is akin to what the author Robert Ringer called the 'Iceball Theory'. In fifty million years when the sun goes out and earth becomes an iceball it won't matter what you did or failed to do aeons and aeons ago; nothing will remain of you or your deeds . . . If you have no dreams to realize, no goals to achieve, no ambition other than to exist until the eternal caravan calls out your name, then OK, you can go along with the iceball theory. But the fact is, you are alive *now* at one of the most exciting times in earth's history. And if you believe there are things worth doing in your one life here on earth, if you do have dreams you long to bring about and accept that you haven't got forever to realize them, why play a quiet, conservative, it-can-wait-till-tomorrow kind of game? Where will that get you? The answer is, nowhere. Chronic procrastination will turn your dreams to dust. Your life will be full of might-have-beens. You will feel you are in a deep rut. Is that *really* how you want to live?

Moreover, if we are in some kind of a rut, chronic procrastination will almost guarantee that we will stay in it! And if we are not already in a rut, persistent procrastinating will almost certainly help us to get into one.

Rationalizations and other escapist devices or avoidances stop us from facing up to difficult problems and they add new difficulties later. The uncompleted tasks remain, the problems remain unsolved and new and greater difficulties emerge. You can see examples of this at every level of society from individuals through companies large and small up to governments themselves. Nothing works except working. If your rationalizations block you from working, from doing NOW, look behind your rationalizations for the irrational beliefs which feed and keep them alive and forcefully dispute them in thought and in action using the techniques we have described in this chapter. Find out by experimenting which ones work best for you and then stick to them. Regardless of how long you have been procrastinating, you actively and consciously can work to undo the procrastination and the defences you erected to protect it. These remarks apply equally well if you find yourself in a rut.

Practically everyone procrastinates at least occasionally, but it becomes a problem when it interferes with productive living. One of us (JG) has devised a two-line verse which he recites to remind himself that individual existence is time-limited and therefore to achieve one's goals in life, one had better make the maximum use of time, of which there is nothing more precious:

Forever I can sit and stew
But I haven't forever to live and do!

We hope we have provided you with some useful ideas you can use to stop procrastinating, and to get out of ruts and start living. If any of you discover new ideas or original techniques to combat procrastination which you find work for you, we shall be pleased to hear from you. We always welcome effective new ideas. Just write to us care of our publisher.

5

'I Need a Quick Fix'

In this chapter we will show how people use 'quick fixes' to avoid discomfort or to feel good or in control of themselves. We will also explain why people act in unproductive ways through the use of quick fixes and why the habitual use of various forms of these quick fixes will almost always do the user harm in the long term. Quick fixes, because they provide a degree of immediate comfort, can quickly become a habit which becomes self-sustaining. This in turn can lead to various forms of addiction which then create their own problems. The end result is a great deal of personal and social misery.

What is a quick fix?

A quick fix is any kind of activity in which an individual indulges in order to overcome a feeling of discomfort and/or to obtain a feeling of comfort or euphoria. For example, a person with a low tolerance of boredom will feel the need for a quick fix to get rid of the negative feelings associated with boredom (eg, 'I can't stand feeling bored') as well as providing a quick route into feelings of pleasure, excitement or a general feeling of euphoria. The particular quick fix employed varies according to individual inclinations. One person may binge on a box of chocolates; another person may swallow two or three large whiskies; another person may pop a couple of Valiums. Almost anything can become a fix; some people become compulsive shoppers (shopaholics) as a temporary means of evading the discomfort caused by a marriage or relationship problem, for example. Others may opt for a complete change of furniture, hoping that this will solve their problem.

Why quick fixes work – in the short term

The one thing all quick fixes have in common is the ability to make you feel good, or to stop you feeling bad, at least for a time. The good feeling may be psychological, or a combination of physical and psychological elements. Alcohol, tranquillizers and certain foods, such as chocolate, possess properties which act on the brain and nervous system to produce the desired physical and psychological effects. These range from the merely pain-numbing to positive feelings of euphoria. Psychological fixes provide comfort through novelty, excitement or diversion – such as watching TV soap operas, which of course, are intended to be addictive.

All quick fixes fulfil two purposes:
1. to enable the user to avoid a dysphoric or uncomfortable state, such as boredom
2. to create a euphoric or pleasurable state, such as joy, elation, etc.

We are not claiming that any of these products or activities are necessarily quick fixes in themselves. Everyone who downs a stiff whisky or two is not necessarily employing the drink as a quick fix any more than anyone who watches a soap opera regularly is necessarily using the TV serial to evade some uncomfortable emotional problem. In order to recognize a quick fix we have to look at the motivation behind it. As we have already stated, quick fixes, because of their quick-acting properties, can soon become addictions which create a whole new set of problems. Although quick fixes are seen by those who use them as the answers to their problems, the truth is that quick fixes are employed essentially as a means of covering up or evading some problem(s) which the quick fix user either refuses to acknowledge, or feels s/he cannot resolve or cope with. For example, if you have lost a close relative or dear friend, the pain of grieving can be so intense that you may lose your appetite, be unable to sleep properly, and lose interest in work and social activities. You may be grateful if your doctor prescribes you Valium to help you sleep better and to dull the pain of grieving, but the pain of losing someone you loved doesn't go away. With or without the tranquillizer, you have to face the reality sooner or later that you are bereaved and that you must come to terms with it before you can get your life back on to an even keel. Having seen why quick fixes work as short term expedients, let us now examine why people are attracted to them and what the long-term consequences are when quick fixes become addictions.

Why people think they need a quick fix

Nobody enjoys being deprived of something they desire. We all experience negative emotions when our wishes are frustrated. The pain of being deprived is real. However, there are degrees of deprivation and the language we use to express our pain at being deprived doesn't always accurately reflect the level of pain we experience. It is a fact that language influences both the way we perceive the world around us, and the way we think and feel. In turn, the way we think and feel influences the language we use to express our thoughts and feelings. For example, a moderately frustrating experience may be perceived quite accurately as irritating or annoying. We wanted something and we didn't get what we wanted. So we are deprived! Too bad! If you told yourself it's too bad and really believed that it was just too bad, but hardly the end of the

87

world, your feeling in response to being deprived would probably be one of disappointment. You would try to overcome your disappointment by seeing what you could do to avoid being frustrated the next time you set out to get what you wanted.

Unfortunately, people don't always respond in such a relatively rational way to the hassles and frustrations which abound in real life. Instead of saying to themselves, 'It's too bad that what I wanted didn't come about', people whine about the 'horror' of being deprived: 'I *can't stand* being deprived of what I want! I *must* have it and it's *terrible* to be treated like this! Life isn't being as *fair* to me as it should!' To ease the pain of being deprived of what they had insisted they must have, and to make up for life treating them so 'unfairly', such people treat themselves to a few stiff drinks, or raid the fridge for a few goodies like a chocolate gateau to stuff themselves with, or they take off on a shopping spree and buy themselves things they don't really need but which 'make them feel good'. But the pleasure one gets from these quick fixes is short-lived – and there's a price to be paid sooner or later, and sometimes it's a high one.

The main point being made here is that the experience of being deprived leads to negative feelings. Negative feelings arise from your perception of being deprived of something or losing something you wanted, something you value. These negative feelings of disappointment, sorrow, or annoyance are uncomfortable but bearable. In fact, they are healthy because they motivate you to take some kind of constructive action. You get yourself into trouble only when you view such negative feelings as 'awful' or 'terrible'; convince yourself that you can't stand the discomfort associated with these 'horrible' negative feelings, and then feel driven to adopt unproductive ways of avoiding your discomfort. These 'quick fixes' may alleviate the discomfort and help you to feel good, but the effects don't last very long.

We will show you presently how various forms of quick fixes can easily become habits which become ritualized and lead to dependency. But first, let's examine those irrational beliefs people bring to situations where they are deprived of something they strongly desire and how their irrational thinking leads to the adoption of various quick fixes to anaesthetize the pain of discomfort and to fulfil the need to feel good.

Irrational beliefs behind the quick fix

We've already mentioned some of the most common iBs people cling to when attempting to justify their resort to quick fixes:
    'I *can't stand* being deprived of what I want!'
    'I *must* have it and it's *terrible* to go without!'

'Life isn't being *fair* to me!'

and then they will frequently add:
'And it *absolutely should* be!'

You may well recognize these irrational beliefs – derivatives of the major irrational belief:
'Because it is preferable that I experience pleasure rather than pain, the world absolutely should arrange this and life is horrible, and I can't bear it when the world doesn't.'

The more strongly you hold that iB, whether you are aware of it or not, the more likely you are to become a habitual quick-fix user – for the simple reason that life doesn't supply us quickly and easily with what we want or grant us freedom from pain or spare us from the vicissitudes, frustrations and hassle which are part and parcel of everyday life.

Eddie was a 27-year-old man whose life resembled a kind of treadmill as he desperately tried to keep one jump ahead of reality, whatever it was – money for cigarettes, booze or sex – he just had to get it, and he would lie, bully, deceive, 'borrow' and steal from friends and relatives alike to get what he insisted he must have. So long as he was earning money and things were going his way he could be charming and generous. However, Eddie would spend all his wages almost within a day or two of receiving them and then survive the remainder of the week by borrowing from relatives and friends. But as inevitably happened, when his demands failed to be met, the result was violent verbal abuse directed mainly at women whom he claimed were frustrating him, accompanied by furniture smashing episodes and outbursts of rage. Theoretically, Eddie was quite capable of looking after himself. He was physically fit and could tackle a number of different manual jobs efficiently and well. But because Eddie clung to the childish demand that the world – and especially his mother and various girl friends – had to treat him well, look after him and always give him what he wanted when he wanted it, he lived on the knife edge of anxiety interspersed with bouts of self-pity and verbal abuse of his associates or friends when they failed to live up to his demands, or simply left him.

Eddie's irrational beliefs are derivatives of the following major irrational beliefs:

'Because it is highly desirable that others treat me considerately and

fairly, they absolutely should and must, and they are rotten people
who deserve to be utterly damned when they do not.'

'I must be comfortable; I shouldn't have to go through too much
discomfort to get what I want; life should be good; if it isn't I can't
stand it!'

If you subscribe only to the latter, this can easily lead you to feel self-
pitying and depressed and is therefore the main generator of the quick
fix; if you also take on board the former irrational belief – as Eddie
undoubtedly had – you have double the chance of making yourself
miserable; for this irrational belief generates intolerance, anger and
hostility. The core belief of 'other people must treat me as I wish, and if
they don't, they're no good and deserve to be damned!' contributes to,
and reinforces the 'I must be comfortable' . . . belief. But since other
people usually have their own lives to lead they will sooner or later tire of
being put upon and will either ignore your dictates or withdraw from
you. When that happens, you then feel the 'need' for a quick fix to help
you get over other people's 'inconsiderate' behaviour towards you.

Quite apart from doing you harm by encouraging you to go for a quick fix
when other people refuse to kow tow to your every demand, the 'other
people must treat me as I wish' belief does nothing for your relationships
with other people, especially your intimate relationships. People who are
constantly demanding this or that, and who easily upset themselves
whenever their demands are not immediately met, are not easy to live with.

Dispute

The irrational belief is:

'Because it is highly desirable that others treat me considerately and
fairly, they absolutely should and must, and they are rotten people
who deserve to be utterly damned when they do not.'

When you challenge and dispute an irrational belief, regardless of the
form it takes, essentially what you are doing is using the scientific method
to question the belief to see whether it gives you healthy results, and
whether it accords with facts, with reality (which can change), and with
logical thinking. Note that science eschews dogma; it avoids rigid all-or-
nothing thinking as well as either/or thinking. Science sees reality as
complex, having many sides to it and following the laws of probability
rather than certainty – especially where human affairs are concerned.

Keeping these criteria in mind, you can challenge any belief by asking
three basic questions of it:

1. Is this belief realistic and factual?

2. Is this belief logical? Or is it self-contradictory and illogical?
3. If I accept this belief will I get good results from it? Will acting on this belief help me to achieve my goals?

These three basic questions or criteria of rationality will enable you to decide in nearly all cases whether a given belief can be rationally upheld. You can, if you wish, add a fourth question to your armamentarium which you may find useful occasionally:

4. Is this belief flexible and non-rigid? Or does it insist that something is unconditionally true under all conditions and for all time?

Science is sceptical of any ideas which lay claim to absolute 'Truth' or 'Certainty'. The scientific method strives for greater truth, for an ever closer approximation to 'reality' but not for 'absolute and perfect truth'. And lastly, if you want to be really scientific, you can ask a fifth question:

5. Can this belief be falsified?

Science has no truck with beliefs or theories which cannot be falsified in some way. If a given statement or belief appears to be fundamentally unfalsifiable, or untestable, it is not scientific!

Generally speaking, you will find the first three criteria adequate for your purpose. Occasionally, depending upon the content of the iB, criteria 4 and 5 can add a bit of extra 'muscle' to your disputing technique.

The disputing sequence
'Because it is highly desirable that others treat me considerately and fairly, they absolutely should and must, and they are rotten people who deserve to be utterly damned when they do not.'

Question 1: Is this belief realistic and factual?
Analysis: No, it insists that other people absolutely should and must treat me considerately and fairly. That means that under all conditions and at all times other people must treat me considerately and fairly. Do they? Obviously not. Moreover, the facts of life prove that often people will not treat me considerately and fairly. Therefore the belief is neither factual nor realistic.
Another point: Is it factual that people who do not treat me considerately and fairly are rotten individuals? Again, the answer is 'No'. Rotten individuals would be rotten to the core, would always do rotten deeds, would virtually be doomed to act rottenly and would have no redeeming features. It is unlikely that such totally rotten people exist.

91

A final point: Do people who treat me inconsiderately and unfairly always deserve to be damned, and presumably punished? Even if I could prove somehow that these people deserved damnation and punishment, does that actually happen in reality? It certainly doesn't! So once again, this belief is neither factual nor realistic.

Question 2: Is this belief logical?

Analysis: No, it doesn't follow that because I desire other people to treat me considerately and fairly, therefore they must do so. Also, even if I could prove that by commonly accepted standards I had been treated inconsiderately and unfairly, it does not logically follow that therefore these people are totally rotten individuals and therefore are utterly damnable.

Question 3: If I accept this belief will I get good results from it? Will acting on this belief help me to achieve my goals?

Analysis: It's very unlikely! If I strongly believe that other people have to treat me considerately and fairly and that they are rotten people who deserve damnation when they fail to treat me as I command, I will in fact get some unfortunate results:

(1) I will so enrage myself that I could endanger my health and if I were to continue to get myself all worked up, I could suffer from cardiovascular problems, one of which might prove fatal.

(2) If I try to talk people into treating me more considerately or fairly, I am liable to enrage myself over their behaviour to such a degree, that they will think I simply want a fight with them, and consequently will either fight back or walk away from me. In either event, they will tend to see me as highly irascible, almost impossible to talk with in a calm, friendly manner, and tend to avoid me as much as possible.

(3) Even if some people deliberately treat me unfairly and inconsiderately, my demanding, condemning attitude will interfere with any hope I have of understanding why they behave in that way, or of non-blamingly discussing with them ways in which I and they might reach a mutually acceptable compromise.

If you have followed our reasoning so far, you will see that this particular irrational belief is unrealistic, is distinctly illogical and if you continued to hold it, you would more often than not sabotage your own interests.

You could go on and apply Questions 4 and 5 (see p. 91) to the analysis we have just offered. For example, you could apply Question 4 and show that this particular iB is rigid, dogmatic and inflexible for it states that without exception all people who treat me unfairly and inconsiderately are entirely rotten people who deserve nothing but damnation.

Similarly, you could apply Question 5 (Can this belief be falsified?) and show that the idea that people who treat me badly are totally rotten individuals is false because it can be shown that these people often do some good or neutral acts. On the other hand, the idea that people who treat me badly 'deserve' utter damnation is impossible to prove. Who can say what one 'deserves'? That idea is probably untestable.

The rational alternative belief

- 'Although it is highly desirable that others treat me considerately they don't have to do so. If they don't, they are not necessarily acting in a deliberately unfair or inconsiderate manner and even if some people deliberately treat me unjustly they are not rotten individuals worthy only of damnation but merely fallible humans carrying out their own agendas for living. While I am displeased when people treat me unfairly I don't have to disturb myself over their poor behaviour. If it is important to me I can bring their inconsiderate or unjust treatment of me to their attention and assertively try to persuade them to behave in ways more acceptable to me. If I succeed, fine. If I don't, I can figure out some way of penalizing their poor behaviour, or I can avoid them altogether.'

We have devoted considerable space to emphasizing the scientific method of analysing and disputing irrational beliefs as shown in the example above because it is one of the main methods we used in 'Rational-Emotive Therapy' (RET) to identify and uproot the main sources of emotional distress. If you practise using this method you will find it a powerful antidote to the beliefs which create the desire for a quick fix as well as the even more damaging dependencies and compulsions which can take over the control of your life once the use of quick fixes becomes a habit. Later in this chapter you will be given plenty of opportunities to explore the application of these disputing techniques to the problems of dependency and compulsive behaviours which take their toll today on the health and happiness of many unfortunate people.

Acknowledge your negative feelings

We've shown you how to spot and challenge the irrational beliefs which push you into a quick fix. It is important to realize that quick fixes are cover-ups for many kinds of real problems. Perhaps you've lost your job; perhaps your marriage is in trouble; perhaps you've lost someone dear to you through death. Such unfortunate or tragic happenings will normally lead to strong negative feelings such as sadness, intense grief, or anxiety and depression. Since negative feelings are unpleasant and uncomfortable, and since they will often persist for quite a long time, the individual experiencing these dysphoric feelings may sometimes succumb to the temptation to get a quick fix in order to get rid of the discomfort and replace it with more pleasurable feelings. The original problem situation is still there, of course, together with those uncomfortable negative feelings accompanying it. But for the moment, the quick fix has taken over and that troublesome problem and its associated uncomfortable feelings can be pushed into the background.

Methods which aim for a healthier and more profound resolution of the individual's basic problem in the longer term need time to work. The quick fix, by contrast, produces its pleasurable effects almost instantaneously. The very speed with which they work can easily blind people to what they really feel. One of the consequences of the quick fix is that some people fail to confront their feelings to find out how they really feel. The ease with which various kinds of quick fix can be obtained beguiles people into thinking that the quick fix is the answer to their problems, whereas the quick fix is merely a palliative to ward off or diminish the discomfort associated with their primary problem.

Find out what you feel!

It is important to get in touch with your true feelings. So long as you cover them up with quick fixes, and fail to acknowledge the nature of your true feelings, you are unlikely to resolve your original problem or to feel that you are in control of your life. In fact, quick fixes will do you in in the long term. Rational thinking may take much longer to work than alcohol or tranquillizers or any other quick fix, but in the long run it's a healthier solution and, if you diligently practise it, will stand you in good stead for the rest of your life.

Why quick fixes make us feel good

Quick fixes have certain properties which provide us with pleasureable feelings. Certain foods appeal strongly to our sense of taste. Chocolate, for example, is almost universally regarded as a very pleasant-tasting substance. Knowing this, chocolate manufacturers specialize in making up all kinds of deliciously tasting chocolates. A friend of ours who is no chocolate lover by any means, and who doesn't even have a 'sweet tooth', needs only to have a certain brand of boxed chocolates put in front of her which she finds so irresistible that she is hard put to stop herself from eating the entire contents at one sitting. Most of us have our favourite foods which can be eaten with enjoyment in moderation. But not always! Another friend of ours can't resist a certain brand of sweetened condensed milk. Once a tin of it is opened, she begs someone to take it away, otherwise she will go on eating and eating it!

As these examples illustrate, food and drink can be a great comforter quite apart from its nutritional value (or lack of it). However, problems begin when the desire to eat – or drink alcohol – for comfort becomes an absolute need – in other words, when eating or drinking becomes a compulsion. As we have already pointed out, underlying emotional problems or dilemmas which remain unresolved are the generators which drive people into adopting one or more kinds of quick fix which can quickly become a compulsive ritual accompanied by all the problems of dependency.

The main kinds of quick fix and what they can do to you

Our aim in this chapter is to draw attention to various non-clinical problems arising from the habitual use of quick fixes, and to show you effective methods for dealing with them. Consequently we will not spend time discussing the treatment of the more serious kinds of compulsive drug abuse which really require clinical treatment. Instead, we shall confine ourselves to just a brief mention of the more tragic consequences which arise when eating, drinking and other kinds of fixes develop into full-blown compulsions. But first, let's discuss the kinds of quick fix which do not involve the ingestion of various substances.

Shopaholicism

As we noted, you can make practically anything into a psychological compulsion. Like gambling and the other fixes discussed later, shopaholicism serves two main purposes: it enables the person to feel good, and it serves to blot out, temporarily, discomfort anxiety about some other primary problem.

Shopaholicism means shopping just for its own sake. Buying the weekly groceries for the family, or new clothes for the children doesn't qualify as shopaholicism. That kind of shopping serves a rational purpose. It is more of a normal routine than a compulsion. The difference is that compulsive shoppers do have a choice about *what* they buy; they believe they do not have a choice about *buying*.

Who are the shopaholics?

Shopaholics are mainly, although not exclusively, women. Our cultural standards and sex roles imply that women do the shopping, not only for themselves, but for their families as well. This is changing to some extent, but a survey of any large supermarket or department store will

95

show that women make up by far the majority of those shopping and/or browsing.

Some typical reasons women give for compulsive shopping:

- 'It fills in time; I can't bear to be doing nothing.'
- 'It gives me a sense of power, a feeling that I am in control and prepared for the unexpected.'
- 'When I shop with a credit card, it feels good because I feel better off than I really am.'
- 'It gets rid of boredom and it can be exciting to splurge out on nice new things.'
- 'When I feel angry with my partner I go shopping and charge it up to him. After all, I buy him presents, so it's a way of evening up the score.'
- 'I feel so lonely at times. It's then that I have to go shopping. At least you're with people and they talk to you.'
- 'I guess it gives my ego a boost when I'm feeling low. Trying out a new perfume, or the latest style in clothes makes me feel a different person.'

These are just some of the reasons some women give for shopping to ease the pain of some unresolved problem in their lives and to enable them to feel good inside for a time. In these circumstances, when shopping is done for emotional, rather than for utilitarian reasons, there is a tendency to spend more than is wise. This is understandable when the motive is to relieve feelings of emotional discomfort and to give oneself an emotional boost, but it is counterproductive since it leads to feelings of guilt or anxiety afterwards. Women realize this, of course, but see no alternative, other than putting up with the pain of discomfort over some perceived lack or deprivation in their lives.

Impatience is in itself a form of quick fix which is often associated with compulsive shopping. The shopper doesn't just want to relieve feelings of boredom, or loneliness, etc.; s/he wants attention now, pronto! The compulsive shopper in search of a quick fix is in no mood to wait patiently in a queue for sales attention. 'I must have X, and I must have it now!' is the overriding thought.

Gambling

As with drinking, eating and drug use, gambling can be a relatively harmless way of providing you with a little bit of pleasure. Gambling is exciting for many people, perhaps for most people. It gives one a 'kick' to put a bet on a race, or to bet on the spin of a roulette wheel, in the knowledge that if you win, you can at least double your money, or even obtain a return many times the size of your original bet. So it's easy to see why gambling has been around for a long time in one form or another. And since most of us have gambled at some time in our lives, even if it was only a few pence each week on the football pools, or a once a year 'flutter' on the Derby, it is hardly surprising that gambling is today a multi-billion pound business.

Since gambling can be exciting, it is particularly attractive as a form of quick fix to people who have a low tolerance of boredom and a need to feel good, to 'feel on top'. Like any other quick fix, gambling can become compulsive. When that happens, gambling can seriously disrupt one's life because of associated monetary problems, employment difficulties, personal and family problems, marital disharmony, and perhaps even legal problems. If gambling has become, or is becoming the be-all of your existence, it is time you sought professional help from a qualified and experienced therapist or treatment agency.

Why some people gamble

We are talking here of inveterate gamblers – individuals for whom gambling has become a way of life. What sort of people are they, these people who gamble daily, compulsively, on horses, on dogs, or in casinos where they can play anything from poker machines through roulette to varieties of poker and blackjack? As with alcohol, facilities to gamble are freely available; gambling is even encouraged by state-run lotteries, while football pools, betting, and bingo games are national pastimes. It is not surprising, therefore, that many people can be drawn to a life of gambling.

Here are some typical characteristics of compulsive gamblers:

- Higher than average IQ
- Good with numbers; they can calculate and remember numbers, results, etc.
- Very competitive: they believe that they have to beat everyone
- A low threshold of boredom
- Low frustration tolerance
- Low self-esteem
- Tend to be non-assertive
- Poor coping skills
- Tend to be ineffective communicators
- Tend to be loners.

The list above is not intended to be comprehensive; however, it does suggest the kind of irrational beliefs one might expect to find among gambling addicts. For people aren't *made* into addicts. As we've already

97

shown you, RET places the responsibility for human disturbance and self-abuse – regardless of whatever form it takes, squarely where it belongs: on the self-defeating individuals themselves. This does not mean that we blame them for their problems. (Far from it, since taking responsibility involves self-acceptance, while blame involves putting the other person down. Nor do we go to the ridiculous extreme of claiming that people are *totally* responsible for *all* their behaviour. They aren't, since we do have impinging on us the very powerful forces of heredity, nutrition, social learning, politics, economics and other biological and environmental conditions. In the case of compulsive gamblers, we have evidence that many of them come from severely dysfunctional families with a history of alcoholism and gambling.) Nevertheless, we do contend that people *largely* disturb themselves, even though several other biological and social factors *contribute* to their disturbances. Not only do we believe that people largely create their own disturbed feelings, but we have a theory about precisely *how* humans disturb themselves and how, consequently, they can think and work at undoing their upset feelings and at *not* disturbing themselves any longer.

The irrational beliefs of compulsive gamblers

Let's now look at the irrational beliefs which drive gamblers on and on until they are no longer in control of themselves. It is not uncommon to find that compulsive gamblers refuse to admit they have a problem. Even when they become the victim of stress-related illnesses, they find if easy to deny that there is anything really wrong with them. In response to the question: 'How are you?' they will answer: 'Oh, I'm fine, just fine!' By the time the compulsive gambler is spending his week's pay cheques on gambling, placing bigger and still bigger bets in a desperate effort to recoup his losses, he will unconcernedly state: 'I don't have a problem!' when it is quite obvious to everyone else who knows what is going on that he *does* have a serious problem.

Interestingly, many compulsive gamblers view money as the solution to all their problems; for them, money buys acceptance. So long as they get acceptance, then the pain of boredom and loneliness can be kept at bay. They are frequently people-pleasers. So, given that information plus the knowledge that compulsive gamblers are extremely competitive, what would you guess might be the motivating iBs?

Here are some typical iBs:

'I *must* be in control at all times, of all things and of all people.'
'I *must* be totally competent!'
'I *must* be liked, loved and appreciated by people who are important to me! If I'm not, that proves that I'm no good.'

98

These iBs are derivatives of the major irrational belief which in its general form states:

'Because it would be highly preferable if I were outstandingly competent and/or loved, I absolutely should and must be; it's awful when I am not, and therefore I am a worthless individual.'

Using the criteria for rationality we set down earlier, can you see that the first part of this irrational belief makes no sense at all? First, does it logically follow that because it is preferable to be highly competent and/or loved, that therefore one should and must be? Obviously it doesn't. Second, is it realistic? Is the belief in accord with the facts of reality? Again, no! For if it were in accord with reality, if there existed a law to that effect, we could all become outstandingly competent and loved on demand! That might be lovely, but it obviously isn't true.

And what about the second part of that iB – that it is awful not being outstandingly competent and/or loved? As we have shown 'awfulness' – when properly defined – is a meaningless term. Let's remind you why it is meaningless. First, awful means bad or very bad; now let's agree that it is very bad if you are not outstandingly competent and/or loved. But to say that it is *awful* means several other things:

(1) that it is *totally* bad that you are having these problems;
(2) that it is more than bad;
(3) that it must not be as bad as it is.

Now, if you think about it, can you claim that it is *totally*, or 100 per cent bad, that you are not outstandingly competent and/or loved? And is it so bad that it couldn't be worse? Obviously it could be worse. You could be dying of an incurable cancer; you could lose your nearest and dearest in a traffic accident or air disaster. Second, 'awful' really means more than bad, more than 100 per cent bad, more than 101 per cent bad. Can anything really be *that* bad? Lastly, 'awful' as applied to our problem of not being competent, etc. really means that it is worse than it should or must be. But however bad it is, it's exactly as bad as it is – and it must be that bad, because it is! Anything that exists, no matter how bad, must be exactly that bad. So, you see, no problem is ever really *awful*.

Similarly, you can dispute the belief that unless one performs outstandingly well and/or is loved and approved of by significant people, then one has no worth, no value, at all. Before you dispute that iB, spare a thought for the case of Ted.

Ted became a compulsive gambler in his twenties. He came from a severely disturbed family, his father being addicted to gambling for as far back as Ted could remember. Ted never saw much of his father; on the relatively few occasions his father was seen with his family, Ted recalled that there would be gifts of toys, or sometimes new clothes or shoes would turn up. Later in life Ted realized that these occasions probably coincided with the times when his father had done well on the race track. But they didn't happen often. When he was a young boy, Ted recalled how his father would put his arm round Ted's shoulders and tell him: 'Be smart, son! When you grow up, go for the big money! And don't trust anybody!' But most of the time Ted remembered hearing only violent rows between his father and mother. He remembers his mother crying a lot and drinking. Then one day, Ted's father was killed in an automobile crash. Ted's brother and sister were shipped off to relatives and Ted was put in an orphanage. His mother had simply given up, she could no longer cope and Ted hardly ever saw his mother after that. Ted soon learned that orphanages were hardly places noted for the lavishing of loving kindness. His few friendships were short-lived. By the time Ted left school he had only one ambition: to make money through gambling. Ted thought maybe his father had not been as smart as he thought he was; or maybe he was just unlucky – probably a bit of both, decided Ted. But Ted was determined to 'go out there and show 'em!' He got himself a job as a cashier with a travel company in the town where he lived.

Ted found horse racing exciting and challenging. Nothing else interested him. It gave him something to do with his life. It gave meaning to his life. Then, one day, after a long run of bad luck during which Ted had come close to bankrupting himself, Ted was caught falsifying his firm's books to generate extra cash to meet his gambling debts.

Don't blame it all on your past!

You might think that Ted could hardly avoid becoming addicted to gambling in view of his unfortunate upbringing. Yet, while Ted's self-destructive behaviour is clearly related to past and understandable causes, these antecedent events in his childhood did not, by themselves, cause Ted's problems, but rather Ted's beliefs *about* the these events and circumstances. External events, such as being mistreated when you were young, may contribute to your emotional and subsequent behavioural reactions, but they do not *cause* your reactions. In the main, *you feel as you think: you create your own feelings by the way you think about and evaluate whatever you perceive is happening to you.* That is *Insight no. 1.*

Insight no. 2 is the understanding that regardless of how you disturbed yourself in the past, *if you are disturbed now, it is because you* still *believe the irrational ideas with which you created your disturbed feelings in the past*, and that you are continuing to actively re-indoctrinate yourself with these unsustainable beliefs, *not* because you were previously 'conditioned' to hold these beliefs and now do so 'automatically', but because you are continually reinforcing these ideas by your present inappropriate actions or inaction, in addition to your unrealistic thinking.

In other words, if, long after your parents or whoever brought you up have ceased to tell you what to think and do, you find you are still behaving in a self-defeating manner, you may suspect that you are still clinging to at least some of the same old nonsensical ideas you easily acquired during your suggestible years in the past. Until you clearly accept responsibility for the continuation of your irrational beliefs, you are likely to make only feeble attempts to dispel them. We're not saying the past is unimportant; what we are saying is that there is no need for you to carry the miseries of the past into your future!

Insight no. 3 is the clear realization and unflinching acknowledgement of the fact that it is your own human tendency to think crookedly that created emotional problems in the past, and that *since these problems have persisted because of self-indoctrination in the present, there is nothing for it except hard work and practice if these irrational beliefs are to be uprooted*, and to remain uprooted until they wither to the point where they cease to be a problem.

One of the most constructive ways of dealing with real-life tragedies, such as the influence of bad family structures and disturbed parental behaviour upon early development, is the repeated rethinking and disputing of family- and society- inculcated irrational beliefs, together with repeated actions designed to undo them. Only by such a double-barrelled attack on one's early acquired irrational beliefs can these beliefs – and the feelings and behaviours resulting from them – be extinguished or their effects minimized.

Let's conclude this section now by returning to the irrational belief which states:

'Unless I am outstandingly competent and loved or approved by people significant to me, I am worthless.'

While this book has focused on problems in dealing with discomfort, the other major problem area with which people have encountered difficulty is in the area of self-worth. While we will consider this briefly here, we recommend an excellent book by our good friend and colleague, Dr Paul Hauck, entitled *Hold Your Head Up High* (Sheldon, 1991) for a comprehensive treatment of this important topic.

Now, let's see how we can dispute the idea that we are worthless if we are not outstandingly competent, loved or have the approval of significant others.

If by 'worthless', you mean worthless to yourself, it follows that you will only feel you have worth, or value to yourself, so long as you are doing outstandingly well. But even if you are *now* doing outstandingly well – just let's suppose that – what guarantee have you that you will be performing outstandingly well tomorrow, and the day after tomorrow, and so on? Since you don't run the universe, how can you guarantee anything? So long as you tie your personal worth to your performance level you will never be free of anxiety; for when you are not performing at your best you will feel miserable; and when you are doing outstandingly well, you will feel anxious about how long you can continue to do well!

In what way are you a worthless person for failing to do well and win the love and approval of others? In *no* way! Even if your acts and behaviour fall far short of your standards, they cannot make *you* a worthless person. Your acts, deeds, performances are only aspects of you; they are never your totality. During your lifetime you will perform literally millions of actions, some good, some bad, some neutral. People may love or approve of you for some of your acts; later, the same people may express only their disapproval of your deeds. What you call *you* consists of innumerable actions, all of which change from day to day, or year to year. You are an ongoing, ever-changing process. How can you then *equal* any of your actions? The products of that process – the products of you – may be evaluated or measured in terms of your goals and values. For example, if you want to train for some competitive sport, such as running or swimming, then it is good if you train hard and win your events, and it is bad if you don't train and do poorly in your events. But *you*, the person, who trains hard or doesn't train hard enough, cannot be given an overall rating. You are you, a process that continually changes, with a past, present and future; and there is no way you can legitimately be measured, rated or given some kind of global rating.

Even if you *never* did anything outstandingly well and never won love or approval from anybody, how could that make you a worthless person? If you were a worthless person, this would mean that you had some *essence*, some soul that was completely worthless, and that you could never do anything worthy of praise or value. Obviously this is unprovable.

By defining yourself as a worthless person when you are behaving inadequately, how will that view of yourself help you to correct your behaviour and do better in the future? The chances are it won't! The

102

more you see yourself as a worthless person, the more will that view handicap you and become a self-fulfilling prophecy. The alternative view is that you are neither a good nor bad person, but a fallible human who does both good and bad acts, but who has the power to act better in the future. Adopt that view, and you will improve your chances of performing more successfully and winning greater approval than if you take on the self-damning view of yourself as having no worth or value at all unless you are performing successfully all the time.

The rational alternative belief.
- 'I would like to perform outstandingly well at certain tasks and win the approval of people I respect, but I don't *have* to. Since, being human, there will be times when I will fail to do well, perhaps even badly, that will be unfortunate and annoying, but hardly awful. I am not a worthless person but a person who sometimes fails to do as well as I'd like and fails to get the results I want. So I'm not infallible. It isn't the end of the world and I can still be fairly happy in spite of my occasional failings, and in spite of the fact that some of those whose approval I valued may now withdraw it. Again, too bad! That's the way it is. Now let me see how I, in spite of these realities, can continue to make the most of my life and enjoy myself.'

If you have a gambling problem, look for and dispute the idea that if you manage to pull off an outstanding win, this makes you an outstanding person. Even if you gain such a win, you are still the same person, and if you think about it, the chance of winning the jackpot is so unlikely that you will see, if you think logically, that it's not worth the heartache and disruption you will, in all probability experience, if you pursue it compulsively.

Eating disorders: bulimia and anorexia

Clinically speaking, bulimia and anorexia are eating disorders. In bulimia, sufferers eat far more than is good for them; they literally stuff themselves with food. Anorexics, on the other hand, resist eating: they literally starve themselves. Bulimia and anorexia are two sides of the same coin; they are both compulsions about food and both compulsions may be present in the same person simultaneously. Bulimics (and in some instances, anorexics) can gorge themselves on various foods over periods ranging from a day to even a week, followed by a cycle of stringent dieting. A compulsive cycle of bingeing and dieting becomes established with potentially serious consequences for the sufferer's health. For some, it becomes virtually a way of life. In several known cases of anorexia, stringent dieting was continued down to starvation levels. Two methods used by bulimia and anorexia sufferers to control their weight following a bout of gorging consists of self-induced vomiting and the frequent use of powerful laxatives. Because being overweight is seen as unbearable, the vomiting and laxatives themselves become quick fixes. Such drastic methods of losing weight can themselves create health problems such as heart palpitations, sweats, and muscle cramps caused by calcium deficiency. Violent swings in weight are not only very debilitating; they can seriously affect physical development, especially in young people in the process of making the transition from adolescence to adulthood. Ironically, the refusal to make that transition, or the determination to reverse it, is the reason offered by some anorexics for rigidly sticking to their starvation diet, in spite of desperate pleas to abandon it from anxious relatives and friends. A few anorexics actually die from self-starvation. For those who survive, life is miserable indeed, characterized typically by bouts of depression, physical illness and sometimes suicide attempts. It is important to remember that whatever form the compulsion may take, and serious though it is, it is not the sufferer's real problem, but a mask for it. *Once the sufferer's underlying main problem has been identified, the compulsion can be seen as an understandable, but highly irrational, response to dealing with the primary problem.*

If you have a weight problem, or think you have, consult a qualified doctor before you go in for some kind of slimming diet, particularly the so-called crash diets. If, despite medical advice against it, you feel an overwhelming urge to diet, punctuated perhaps by periodic spells of bingeing on your favourite foods, you may well have an underlying emotional problem for which you would be well advised to seek professional help from a qualified counsellor who specializes in eating disorders.

Alcoholism

When drinking becomes an overwhelming need for someone, he or she is said to be suffering from alcoholism. In some quarters, alcoholism is seen as a disease for which the only cure is total abstinence. For our part, we see alcoholism as a secondary problem, as 'a way of getting through the day' when the afflicted individual is beset by problems which seem to him or her to be insoluble, and cannot be thought about. The facts are that some 96 per cent of the population drink alcohol at some time or other. The frequency of drinking ranges from an occasional glass of wine or sherry, or a whisky before dinner, to several pints of beer per day. Wine is also consumed today on an ever-increasing scale. The production, marketing and distribution of wine is now carried out on a global scale. The drinking of alcoholic beverages is encouraged also through widespread advertising. A few societies prohit alcohol on religious grounds, but in most countries, and in virtually all industrialized countries, alcohol is easily obtainable and is drunk in sufficiently large quantities to constitute an important source of revenue for many national governments. As a means of maintaining consumption, the tax on alcoholic beverages is carefully set at a level at which the selling price will bring in a substantial amount of revenue without deterring the consumer from purchasing the product.

However, the popularity of alcohol consumption is not due to the widespread availability of alcohol beverages or to their generally affordable price, although these factors obviously play a part. The main reason for the popularity of social drinking is that we find it pleasurable to drink; it gives us a 'lift'. It isn't the taste of alcoholic drinks which gives us those pleasant feelings; the taste for alcoholic beverages is something of an acquired taste. But once you do acquire the taste – beware! For alcohol is a poison. The active ingredient is ethyl alcohol. When swallowed, alcohol soon passes into the bloodstream via the stomach walls and quickly carries out its main function: it depresses the action of our body cells. Taken in sufficient quantity the depressive action of ethyl alcohol can close down all vital activity; you can literally drink yourself to death. There are recorded cases of people who have died, usually unintentionally, through imbibing an overdose of alcohol. So why do we drink the stuff?

Most people when they drink are looking for just that amount of alcohol in their bloodstream which will give them a pleasant relaxed feeling – a mood change is what they seek. In these comparatively small doses, the effect of alcohol is most noticeable on our brain cells, especially those cells in that part of the brain responsible for judgement, self-control and concentration. By anaesthetizing the brain cells in those areas, alcohol enables people to feel less inhibited, more spontaneous, more talkative, more friendly and more risk-taking. Go to a party when the alcohol is flowing freely and you'll see what we mean! Any doubts or worries one may have had prior to drinking tend to diminish, even to appear pointless or unnecessary. In short, alcohol makes us feel good by working directly on our nervous system.

If these pleasant mood changes were the only effects of alcohol on the human body, alcohol would be simply a relatively harmless recreational drug. Unfortunately, the speed with which alcohol can produce its affects encourages people who feel low to go in for regular and frequent 'top-ups'. This is why alcohol is particularly popular as a quick fix. The idea is that if a little of this stuff can make me feel this good, maybe still more of it will help me feel even better! But alcohol is a drug, and the more often you use it the more you come to depend on it. Your body cells adapt to alcohol, they build up a tolerance to it. This means that you need to drink more and more just to reach the 'high' you would have been able to achieve in the past with just two or three measures of your favourite 'tipple'. The end result of that process if continued long enough is physical and mental deterioration.

Tranquillizers

We are talking here of the minor tranquillizers, drugs which belong to the benzodiazepine family and which came into use in the 1960s as a 'safe' replacement for the barbiturates which had previously been prescribed for many ailments until it was found that barbiturates had strong intoxicating qualities and could be addictive. It was easy to overdose on barbiturates. All these undesirable properties were discovered *after* these barbiturate-based preparations had been in use for some considerable time. You could be forgiven if you tend to respond sceptically to claims made these days for the latest 'wonder drug' or 'happiness pill', guaranteed to banish your worries and make your life sunny and bright without any unpleasant side-effects. With the introduction of these wonderful new drugs with seductive names like Librium, Valium and Mogadon, it wasn't long before doctors were writing, literally, millions of prescriptions for patients with problems of anxiety, depression and insomnia. All they had to do was to swallow the prescribed number of pills and they would feel better. And of course they did – for a time. The after-effects weren't too bad, either. You might feel a bit sluggish, a bit slow to get started the next morning as you went about your business, but these effects soon passed. It was certainly better than alcohol with its nasty hangovers and the nausea of having drunk one too many or of mixing your drinks.

To be fair, one can hardly blame the patients for going on to Valium and its sister drugs. After all, the doctor said they were all right, and if the doctor said it was OK for us to take these pills who were we to question? Moreover, these pills made us feel good and to be fair to the doctors, hadn't they been assured by the drug companies that these new drugs had none of the bad side-effects associated with the barbiturates and were quite safe to prescribe? Besides, the average doctor is a qualified medical practitioner whose expertise lies in diagnosing and finding a cure for our physical ailments; s/he is not a couples counsellor or a trained psycho-therapist. Yet, here were people coming to the doctors' surgeries worried sick about all sorts of personal problems, unable to sleep because of their worries and finding it more and more difficult to manage a home or hold down their job.

Presented with psychological and social problems day in and day out ranging from delinquent children to runaway spouses and burgeoning debt, what could the doctor confronted with it all be reasonably expected to do? If a prescription for sleeping pills or a course of antidepressants could enable the patient to cope better with his or her personal and family problems, why not prescribe what the patients needed to help them through to another day? No doubt the overstretched social services would be involved too and doing their best. In these circumstances the doctors could be forgiven for taking the view that *not* sending their 'problem' patients away with a handful of tranquillizers would only make these patients feel worse, and less able to manage their difficult life circumstances.

Obviously it would be better if the doctors could sit down with the patient and find a way of dealing with the problems which brought them into the surgery in the first place. But with numerous other patients queuing up in the waiting rooms and with only a limited amount of time available to diagnose and deal with their complaints, writing a prescription for tranquillizers must have seemed the only feasible answer.

Then in the early 1980s warnings on dependence began to appear on the labels for the first time. Following years of being on tranquillizers, some people *did* become dependent. Like alcohol, the benzodiazepine tranquillizers depress cell function and after a period of continual usage the patient develops a physical tolerance for the drug, just as others develop a physical tolerance for alcohol. Thus, to obtain relief from the pain of discomfort, the user of tranquillizers has to take ever-larger doses of the drug. The end result is dependence accompanied by withdrawal symptoms when the user attempts to discontinue usage of the drug in order to escape from the tranquillizer trap. Most people can come off tranquillizers under medical supervision without suffering too much from withdrawal symptoms, but the longer you go on taking a drug, the more likely you are to have problems with withdrawal. Moreover, on top of the problem with withdrawal, you still have to resolve the basic problem which you feel was the cause of you taking tranquillizers in the first place: grieving over the loss of a loved one; depression over losing your job and being unable to find another one; anxiety over your ability to maintain your mortgage repayments; a continual worry over the apparently unending ill-health of your child, and so on.

So far, we have been discussing quick fixes which rely on the ingestion of various substances. In fact, you can become psychologically addicted to virtually anything that supplies you with instant relief from the pain of being deprived of whatever it is you think you must have. Whether or not you also develop a physical craving for your quick fix depends upon the way in which it interacts with your nervous system. Your best bet, therefore, if you have some kind of emotional problem such as anxiety or depression, is to frankly acknowledge it and to accept that however uncomfortable it may be to feel anxious or depressed, it is bearable. And your basic problems can be treated. You can also remind yourself that it is one thing to have, say, a problem of anxiety or depression to deal with; it is quite another thing to burden yourself additionally with a drugs or drinking problem as well! It may be hard work to re-examine and try to change your life, but in the long run it will be even harder for you if you don't.

Overcoming your quick fixes

Here are a number of methods you can use to help yourself break free from your quick fixes. Study them carefully, then try some of them out. In addition, we will suggest a number of constructive ways of comforting yourself to replace the destructive ways inherent in the quick fixes you are in the process of giving up. In the long term, of course, the best advice we can offer you is to *identify and acknowledge the basic problem which lies behind your perceived need for a quick fix*. That problem may be boredom, loneliness, a bad relationship or whatever. While you are getting help with that, either by using this book, or by seeking professional help from an agency, you can tackle your propensity to seek a quick fix in a number of ways. Once you overcome your perceived need for a quick fix you will be in a better position to deal with your underlying problem. Now, let's outline some useful techniques for breaking free from those unhealthy quick fixes; then we'll suggest several constructive ways in which you can enjoy yourself in a healthy manner while you work on your original anxiety which helped to drive you to addiction in the first place.

Cognitive methods

We've already shown you in detail how to use cognitive, or thinking methods, to identify and dispute the irrational beliefs which drive people into seeking the comfort of a quick fix. So, rather than go over the same ground again, we will briefly describe another cognitive method you can use in addition to the one you are already familiar with. It is called, 'referenting' (see also pp. 78–9).

Referenting

This is a technique you can use to encourage yourself, or someone else, with a compulsion (eg alcohol or overeating, or some other addiction) to give up their self-defeating behaviour. What you do is to write down a list of the disadvantages of indulging in the undesired behaviour and a list of the advantages of *not* engaging in this activity.

For example, with alcohol addiction, you could list under disadvantages: health problems (such as overweight, insomnia, loss of memory, partial or complete sexual impotence, diabetes and long-term cirrhosis of the liver leading possibly to premature death); money problems; job difficulties; relationship problems and marital breakups. Review your lists several times a day to remind yourself, or whoever needs to, of the value of giving up the compulsions or phobic avoidances. It's a good idea to check the agreed upon referenting lists and see that they are read *regularly*. Print up the lists in large letters and pin the lists on a wall or desk where they can be easily seen, and are difficult to avoid.

Emotive-evocative methods

Rational-emotive imagery

This is a technique we described in Chapter 1 (see pp. 18–21).

Forceful self-dialogue

Here, for example, the substance abuser has a very forceful dialogue with her-/himself, with the irrational voice being actively and vehemently argued against by the rational voice. The dialogues can be recorded on a cassette and listened to, and a check made to ensure that the rational voice does indeed have rational content and that rational arguments are vigorously and convincingly presented. Forceful self-dialogues, when effectively carried out, can help to break up the self-delusions many alcoholics have about their ability to 'manage' their drinking problem without actually stopping it.

Behavioural methods

Stimulus-control

To carry this out effectively, the addicted person rigorously stays away from similar friends and associates, from bars and drug pushers, and avoids people and places likely to tempt him/her into going back to addiction. This is continued until the addiction disappears.

Reinforcements and penalties

In this combined technique, the addict contracts to allow himself to do something enjoyable, such as going on a much desired holiday, or any other strongly desired activity – *except* the addiction of course – only *after* he has refrained from taking the addictive substance on a given day. This is additionally effective if combined with a stiff penalty which is incurred very shortly after an addictive substance is taken. It is best for some reliable person to monitor these procedures to ensure that they are rigorously carried out, rather than leave it to the addict himself. People with strong addictions are *not* reliable self-monitors.

Here is a method shopaholics can use to overcome their compulsive shopping, but which is not applicable to other forms of addiction involving substance abuse: if shopaholicism is your problem, what you do is to permit yourself to shop for some desired item only *after* you have stopped impulsive shopping for a minimum period, say a fortnight, or even longer. The desired item must be a realistic and justifiable purchase, something you would normally buy for yourself sooner or later. As the purchase is made, you can allow yourself to feel good about what you are doing. You can tell yourself you are in control now. You don't feel apprehensive about the consequences. You know you can afford it, so you will suffer no regrets later. If you continue with this plan, resisting all impulsive shopping urges, your controlled shopping will take over from your earlier impulsive shopping as you realize that the former brings pleasure without regret, while impulsive shopping brings you only momentary pleasure but with painful feelings of guilt afterwards.

Healthier substitutes for your quick fix

We are now going to suggest a number of activities you can take up which will provide you with healthier substitutes than the quick fixes you felt driven to previously. These activities are basically distractions and they serve the purpose of providing you with excitement, interesting challenges, companionship and amusement so that you derive some pleasure from life without getting into quick fixes.

What you decide to take up will depend to some extent upon your age and general level of fitness, as well as your particular interests. Thus, if loneliness has been your problem, there are any number of social clubs you can join, from photography clubs to art and drama classes. If you are an outdoor type, you could join the local ramblers association, a good many members of which tend to be single or unattached. If you are more of a sports enthusiast, you can consider hill walking, pony trekking, horse riding, and, for the more energetic, mountain climbing. If you are after excitement, you can consider canooeing, water skiing, white-water rafting and the more demanding black-water rafting. And if you are the really adventurous type, you could try hang-gliding, parachute-jumping and sky-diving. All of these activities can help wean you away from artificial fixes and enable you to consider what you really want out of life and what you need to change to accomplish your goals. You might even find that you have a real talent for one of these sports and become a devotee of it for its own sake. The old saying, 'Nothing ventured, nothing gained!' is as true here as ever. So, go ahead, and venture!

If you are feeling very uncomfortable, then various healthy, self-soothing exercises can help. Thus, you might take a nice warm bath, listen to some relaxing music, practise relaxing exercises, engage in some pleasant mental imagery, ask your partner for a back rub or a cuddle. And you can even hug that old teddy bear that you still have from your childhood. Don't be ashamed to engage in such activities. While they won't change the philosophies that underpin your dire need for comfort, they will satisfy your healthy desire for comfort and won't give you the problems that your quick fixes normally lead to.

6

Change Involves Beating the Comfort Trap

In this final chapter we will focus on the issue that personal change involves discomfort. It would be nice if we could change without any discomfort at all; but alas, the reality is different. Look back at the previous chapters and you will see all the various 'justifications' people provide themselves with to avoid doing what they really want to do because they find it uncomfortable to act, to get started, but are loath to admit it:

> 'I'm not in the mood right now.'
> 'I'll do it tomorrow.'
> 'I have to feel comfortable first.'
> 'I have to feel confident it will turn out right.'
> 'It's *too* hard!'

and so on.

As if overcoming the discomfort involved in personal change was not enough to keep you occupied, personal change also involves hard work. Change is not easy. It is especially difficult, for example (as you will see presently) when your efforts to change some unhealthy habit are inhibited by uncomfortable – and wholly unnecessary – feelings of shame or embarrassment. Change means changing the way you think, feel and act so that you break old habit patterns and develop new ones. It's like beginning a physical fitness programme. When you begin, you tend to feel more comfortable staying the way you are; exercising muscles you have been unaccustomed to using for a considerable time often feels difficult and uncomfortable. But if you persist with your exercises you will find them getting easier, even enjoyable after a time, and you will begin to feel the benefits of your hard work. In the following pages we will explain what is involved in personal change, and we will equip you with a number of powerful techniques which, if you learn and use them diligently, will greatly assist your own efforts to achieve personal change and to maintain it.

Recognize you have a discomfort problem

Who amongst us has not, at some time or other, used one or other of these excuses to dodge an obligation, or to get out of doing some task which we know had better be done *pronto*, but which involves some discomfort, at least to start with? Nobody! The dire need for comfort is well-nigh universal. This is a great pity, because once the idea: 'I have to be comfortable at all times' takes hold of us, then we're really in the Comfort Trap. Being in the Comfort Trap is a great way to fritter life away. And unless the trap is sprung, any great dreams or ambitions or goals will remain unfulfilled, just pie in the sky which will rapidly become a fading memory. 'Someday' is already here.

Taking the easy way out may be more comfortable for you in the short term, but the trouble is that *the easy way out is often the easy way out of the most rewarding life.*

Consider just two examples of how your discomfort problem can stop you from getting what you want in the long term. Suppose that you want to lose weight, but refuse to go through the self-discipline of going on a sensible diet and sticking to it. You will seemingly be taking the easy way out because you will enjoy eating those fattening foods you've got used to and which you want to continue eating. But eventually you won't enjoy carrying around those extra pounds, having to buy larger size clothes, feeling tired and listless much of the time, and risking several ailments that often go with being overweight. Or, when you left school, you may have wanted to go on to study for a degree, or get yourself a professional qualification, but found the studying took up so much of your time that you had to give up other recreational pursuits you particularly enjoyed. So you abandoned your studies and settled for a job that gave you enough cash to get by each week, but with no real prospects of achieving the standard of living you were originally aiming for. It's the same story in the end: the 'easy' or undisciplined way out of life difficulties and responsibilities proves actually harder in the long run and it turns out considerably less rewarding as a result.

Practising avoidance to get round, but not solve, your life problems is only one aspect of the Comfort Trap. In the previous chapter, you saw how seeking out unhealthy ways of comforting yourself whenever uncomfortable feelings pushed themselves into the forefront of your mind, could lead to much worse feelings of discomfort in the long term than any short-term pleasure you might obtain. We called these unhealthy ways of comforting 'quick fixes'.

How to accept yourself with your discomfort problem

When we say, 'accept yourself with your discomfort problem', we mean two very important things:

- First, stop putting yourself down for having the problem! Regardless of the nature of your problem – alcoholism, drug addiction, shopaholicism, whatever – you are *not* a worthless person for having the problem. Having the problem has real, serious disadvantages for you in its own right without you making it worse by denigrating yourself for having got yourself into a fix.
- Second, give up any and every kind of self-rating. Accept yourself *unconditionally*. When you behave badly in some aspect of your life you have not suddenly become a louse; and when you perform well in some other area you do not instantly become a noble or worthy person. *If you tie your personal worth to some aspect of yourself, your worth goes up and down like a yo-yo*. For when you do well, you will esteem yourself, and when you fail to do well, you are bound to disesteem yourself.

Now, let's apply these two principles to a typical problem. Let's say, for example, that you have a problem of alcoholism, and that it has become public knowledge. People are openly criticizing you, thinking badly of you, and are deriding you as a good-for-nothing. You are aware of all this and you feel ashamed. When you feel ashamed of yourself for having displayed some weakness or failing in public, where do you think your shame comes from? It isn't your poor behaviour that makes you feel ashamed. No, *your shame comes from your agreeing with the negative evaluations these others are making of you as a* person. Your detractors are not merely drawing your attention to your poor behaviour; they may be quite right about your behaviour. What they are saying is that *you* are no good for behaving badly, for having an alcohol problem! Well, that may be their opinion, but do you have to go along with it and make it your opinion?

The answer is, certainly not! In fact, you need never feel ashamed of *anything*. Why? Because shame stems from an irrational belief which takes the form:

'I must not reveal a personal weakness in public.'
'I must not be disapproved of by others'.

Then, when people do, in fact, see that you display a weakness in public and denigrate you for having that weakness, you agree with their negative opinions! That's where your shame comes from; you begin with the demand that you must not reveal a personal weakness in public and be disapproved of; then you jump to the self-defeating conclusion that you are a weak or worthless character for having revealed your 'shameful' weakness in public. You tell yourself:

'My goodness! they're right, I am a worthless clod for revealing my weakness!'

With these ideas, you can hardly avoid feeling ashamed or embarrassed, because as you know by now, *your feelings come from your ideas*. It follows that if you want to change your feelings of shame, you have to change the ideas which create it.

What could you rationally believe, assuming that you have a real problem such as alcoholism, which has become public knowledge and is attracting adverse comment addressed to you personally? Your first step in establishing rational convictions about anything is to look for and weed out any irrational ideas which are hindering the emergence of a rational outlook. Thus, in this case, you would take those irrational ideas which we showed you are creating your feelings of shame, and then, using the criteria for rationality which we outlined in Chapter 5 (see pp. 90–1) convince yourself – by using the disputing techniques at your disposal – that these ideas cannot rationally be upheld.

Your purpose in doing so is not simply to eliminate your feelings of shame in order to accept yourself, but because *feelings of shame interfere with and block any efforts you may make to eliminate your alcohol dependency problem*. You can seldom correct self-defeating behaviours until you accept yourself fully. That is why shame is an inappropriate emotional response; it does you in by preventing you from seeing the real cause of your problem and from doing anything effective to resolve it. Since you have already admitted that your alcohol dependency – your alcoholic 'quick fix' – is creating problems for you which are sabotaging your best long-term interests, it obviously makes sense to deal with your shame *about* your alcoholism, before you tackle the problem of alcohol dependency itself.

Disputing your shame-creating beliefs

The target iBs here are:
    'I must not reveal a personal weakness in public.'
    'I must not be disapproved of by others.'
    'I'm a worthless person for revealing my weakness.'

Now, take the first iB above and ask yourself: 'Why *must* I behave as I demand?' There really is no reason, is there? If there was some 'must' governing your acts, you would be unable to act against your 'must'. But you have, in fact, revealed a personal weakness in public; you have, therefore, acted against your supposed 'must'. You have done what you demanded you must not do. It follows that your 'must' has no basis in reality. It exists – along with your 'shoulds' and 'got tos' – only in your head!

Similarly, you can show yourself that the second belief above, 'I must not be disapproved by others' has zero validity for exactly the same reasons.

Your conclusion at the third iB above – 'I'm a worthless person for revealing my weakness!' – can also be questioned: 'Why am I a worthless person because I do stupid things?' Answer, no one, including you, can be a worthless person since it is next to impossible to rate complex human beings in a global way. A person is an organism, an ongoing living process, who performs many acts, some good, some bad, some neutral, and there is no way a person can be given *any* kind of overall evaluation or rating.

Once you have convinced yourself that your previously held beliefs about shame are irrational, you will begin to see that nothing is truly shameful in the world; although many acts and ways of behaving, such as alcohol abuse, have their distinct disadvantages, and had therefore better be avoided, you never have to put your *self* down, even when you behave very foolishly and know that others disapprove of you for behaving in this fashion. Your foolish or self-defeating behaviour only makes you a person who has acted foolishly or self-defeatingly. It never makes you a truly foolish individual, or an individual who can only and always act in a self-defeating manner.

The rational alternative to shame

If you conscientiously work through the disputing process and surrender your shame-creating ideas, you will arrive at a more rational philosophy which will lead you to feel *regret*, rather than shame, when you act foolishly or inappropriately in public. Thus you will tend to believe:

- 'I don't like the fact that I've been acting foolishly in public and the fact that others may be thinking badly of me, but there is no reason why I must not have acted in this way, and there is no reason why people must not think badly of me. It is a pity that this has happened, but it isn't terrible, and I choose to accept myself as a fallible human being who has behaved foolishly or self-defeatingly but who doesn't have to keep on doing so. Now let me see how I can act in more appropriate ways in future and help myself to get more of what I want out of life and less of what I don't want.'

To sum up this section, read and digest these words:

- No self-downing, no self-blame of any kind is legitimate, no matter how many people criticize you. By all means criticize your acts, deeds and performances, but never your self.

- Make an anti-self-rating philosophy your own. Accept that you are error-prone, never perfect.
- Strive to do well, not for ego-raising reasons, but for the enjoyment you derive from doing something well, and to have a better existence.
- You can always accept your *self* no matter how poor your behaviour, and by not giving that much of a damn what other people think. There is *no* other way to get self-acceptance. After all, that's what self-acceptance really means: to thine own self be true!

Putting yourself down, which is a major part of shame, is never necessary. Weigh the real consequences of your acts and if they are unacceptable, strive to do better next time. You can seldom make logical decisions or correct the consequences of your past errors until you accept yourself fully.

Preparing yourself for change

Assuming you have come with us so far, you have acknowledged you are in the Comfort Trap. You also know why you are in the Comfort Trap, you know you have a discomfort problem and you know what kind of discomfort problem it is. And lastly, you accept yourself with your problem; you don't like having it and you wish you had never got yourself into the Comfort Trap in the first place, but, at least, you are not denigrating yourself, putting yourself down, for having a discomfort problem. And, most importantly, you are determined to change – to break clear of the Comfort Trap and stay clear of it. So what comes next? Well, the next necessary step is a clear understanding of the three stages of change and the purpose of the change process. We will take you through each stage and show you why it is essential for you to negotiate successfully each step in the three-stage process if you are ever to break out of the Comfort Trap and stay out.

The purpose of the three stages of change

The purpose of the three stages of change is not just to enable you to solve your discomfort problem, but also to encourage you to develop a *long range* hedonistic philosophy. Merely showing you how to avoid your avoidances, or abandon your quick fixes, would be like providing you with a powerful means of locomotion but without a map showing you your destination and how to get there. So, before we get down to a detailed consideration of how to tackle the three stages of change, let's clarify the overall purpose of change.

117

In Chapter 1 we explained the difference between short-range and long-range hedonism and we suggest you re-read that section if you need to remind yourself of that important distinction. Humans are basically hedonistic in that we seek to stay alive for as long as we can and to achieve a reasonable degree of happiness during our lifetime. We favour long-range hedonism because it yields better results. We teach people to go for both the pleasure of the moment *and* the pleasure of the future, rather than sacrifice more important future gains for immediate gains or gratification. Long-range hedonism is the opposite of low frustration tolerance (LFT). Low frustration tolerance encourages us to go for immediate gratification. Immediate gratification, or short-range hedonism is not necessarily, or always, self-defeating, but it easily becomes a habit which can sabotage our best long-term interests and lead us to experience *less* pleasure in the long run. By all means enjoy yourself but not at the expense of deeper and more rewarding commitments. It has been found through the ages that the short-range hedonistic philosophy of: 'Eat, drink and be merry, for tomorrow you may die', is unrealistic, and therefore irrational; because most of the time you *don't* die tomorrow. Instead you are much more likely to live long enough to rue the consequences of too much eating, drinking and merrymaking today. Often the saner, more rational course to follow (as Freud too, pointed out) is to postpone present pleasures for future gains rather than striving *only* for present gains or gratifications. So, with this in mind, let us consider the three stages of change.

The three stages of change

Stage 1: You can change how you feel and think

You know by now that certain irrational beliefs lead to your discomfort problems. Each chapter so far has identified the relevant irrational thoughts and shown you how to challenge and dispute them so that you give them up. We hope that each chapter gave you insight into how your acquisition of certain widely held iBs put you in the Comfort Trap. Did that insight alone enable you to spring the Comfort Trap so that you are now an autonomous individual confidently conducting your own existence? It's unlikely! Most people 'see' quite quickly when they are shown how they are responsible for their own disturbance, that their self-defeating thoughts, feelings and behaviours create their emotional problems, rather than other people or social conditions. Yet, somehow that insight doesn't instantly dispel their problems. Even knowing that one keeps on believing deep down inside one's early-acquired irrational beliefs, despite 'knowing' that these iBs cannot rationally be upheld, still leaves one's problems largely intact. Obviously, intellectual insight isn't enough.

It isn't enough because our iBs have usually been around a long time. They have become an habitual part of our daily thinking. They are probably part and parcel of our core values. They strongly influence the way we look at the world and evaluate what happens to us. To change ingrained ways of thinking and the habitual reactions which are linked to them, requires effort and much persistent practice.

Stage 1, therefore, consists in acknowledging that your self-defeating behaviour has well-rooted antecedent but understandable relations to events in your past, but that these early events contributed to, but did not cause your problems. Rather, your beliefs about these past events created your problems. In the main, you created your own feelings by the way you thought about and evaluated whatever you perceived was happening to you. And the reason it is difficult to give up old ways of thinking and acting is because human beings are born with a distinct proneness to create their own emotional disturbances; and then as they grow older, they learn to exacerbate and consolidate that proneness through social and cultural conditioning. So change isn't easy, but that doesn't mean it's impossible.

Stage 2: You can break the influence of the past

No matter how you first became disturbed or how poor an upbringing you may have had, you were not conditioned or moulded to think, feel and behave the way you do today, and therefore you are not powerless to change yourself. Obviously, other things being equal, you will have a harder time trying to overcome a severely dysfunctional upbringing than a less severe one. However, you do have the ability to change; we all have that ability. Although, as stated above, we are innately prone to think irrationally, to be self-destructive instant gratification seekers or short-range hedonists, to shirk responsibility and repeat our mistakes over and over again and to be dogmatic, grandiose, intolerant and superstitious, we also, on the other hand, have a tendency to think rationally, to have a powerful predisposition to preserve our lives, to seek pleasure and to avoid pain, and to learn from our mistakes.

We are at our most suggestible state when we are young, which is why our dysfunctional ways of thinking, feeling and behaving usually become established then. Although we tend to remain more or less gullible as we grow older, we are probably better able to use our inborn capacity to think rationally as we acquire experience of living. If our irrational beliefs continue to plague us, it is not because they have some magical ability to sustain themselves, like vagrants without any visible means of support. No, and this is our central point, our iBs persist because we actively reindoctrinate ourselves with them and continually reinforce them by present day inappropriate behaviours. In other words, it is because people are actively and currently propagandizing themselves with their early acquired and more recently borrowed irrational ideas that their disturbed emotions and inappropriate behaviours hold sway over their lives in the present.

Stage 3: It's time for action, work and self-discipline

Once you understand how you originally acquired, and have continued to maintain, your dysfunctional emotions and behaviours, the next question you will want to ask is: 'How do I train myself to change or eliminate my self-defeating beliefs and habits which are still getting in the way of my achieving a better quality life?'

The answer to your question is: 'You can train yourself to undo these self-defeating beliefs and habits which are currently besetting you by self-reconditioning', but this requires self-discipline (which we humans are not born with, but can acquire) plus hard work and practice at understanding, contradicting and acting against irrational belief systems. Irrational beliefs were not born yesterday, they are rooted in the past, many of them with long histories. Consequently, since these irrational beliefs and the problems to which they gave rise have persisted, there is nothing for it except hard work and practice if these iBs are to be uprooted and allowed to wither away to the point where they cease to be a problem for you. In effect, that means repeated rethinking and vigorous disputing of all your irrational beliefs together with repeated actions, specifically targeted upon these iBs and designed to undo them. That is what is necessary if these beliefs are to be extinguished or at least minimized.

We will now move on to detail a variety of cognitive, emotive and behaviour-modification methods designed to help you change the way you have previously been conducting your life. We'll consider the cognitive methods first.

Cognitive methods of change

You will already be familiar with the main cognitive method (disputing irrational beliefs) which we have outlined in each chapter of this book. You will have had some experience of seeking out your irrational beliefs and challenging and disputing them until you see that they make no sense whatever, and then replacing them with more rational alternative convictions. You will know which criteria to apply to determine if a given belief can be considered rational or irrational. Thus, you have a powerful technique at your disposal to enable you to combat *any* irrational beliefs which may try to sneak back from time to time to cause you more misery.

If you want to keep a garden free of weeds, you have to be constantly on the look-out for them; then, when you spot them, you pull them up by the roots. Treat your irrational beliefs like unwanted weeds. On the other hand, your new rational beliefs, which are striving to gain a foothold in your mind, are like young plants or seedlings. If you want them to flourish, you have to nourish them, feed them, and support them until they are strong enough to stand on their own.

The object of these horticultural metaphors is to focus your attention on three vital points. To:

1. *Vigorously combat your irrational beliefs.* The 'softly, softly' approach doesn't work here. Vigorously challenge your irrational ideas many times. If you do, there's little doubt that you can give up the nonsense you've stuck with all those years. You accepted it in the past, and perhaps you had little choice then. But today, you are in the saddle. You don't *have* to cling on to the 'shoulds', 'oughts' and 'musts' that have brought you so much turmoil in the past. There's no insight that works by itself. You either reiterate a belief (and thereby keep it alive), or you vigorously combat it.
2. *Strongly attack your irrational beliefs frequently.* The more frequently you do so, the sooner you will acquire real conviction that they are completely unbelievable. It's easy to dispute iBs in parrot fashion. That is what newcomers to RET tend to do. They see that their iBs don't make sense, but they 'see' it only lightly. They will say to us: 'Yes, I understand what you are saying, and it makes sense, but . . .' Yet, deep down inside, they still cling to iBs such as that they absolutely must be loved and approved, that it's awful if they are not, and so on, and so forth.
3. *Add persistence to the vigour and frequency of your disputing techniques.* Don't give up after a few days and think that that will be enough. Remember that your earlier 'programming' took place over a number of years, so it is unlikely that you are going to dismantle it in the space of a week or two. That simply means that you are going to have to work and practise for as long as it takes for your new rational philosophy to sink in, and truly become a part of you.

To augment your main cognitive method of challenging your irrational beliefs up using the disputing techniques we've taught throughout this book, we suggest you also use *referenting*, a cognitive technique which we described in Chapters 4 and 5 (see pp. 78–9 and 109). This method is particularly useful if your discomfort problem is one of substance abuse.

'How will I know when my new rational outlook is beginning to take root?' you may ask. The answer is: by observing how you feel and behave – especially in situations where you previously tended to feel upset and behaved inappropriately. If you now find yourself coping adequately in these situations, fine. That is encouraging. You are on the right road. But keep working, keep practising! Remember, Rome wasn't built in a day!

Emotive methods of change

We have already introduced you to *Rational-Emotive Imagery* (REI) and given you an example of its use in Chapter 1. Study REI again and see if you can use it to combat some inappropriate feeling that is causing you a problem. For example, are you ashamed about something? You know how to cognitively dispute the iBs underlying shame. You can now reinforce your cognitive disputing by employing REI to still further undermine the idea that you have to feel ashamed because, for example, you needlessly waste money on shopaholic sprees, or because it has become common knowledge at work that you have a drinking problem.

In Chapter 5 we introduced you to a technique known as *Forceful Self-Dialogues*. To give you a more vivid idea of what a forceful self-dialogue sounds like, study the excerpt below. If your discomfort problem is shopaholicism or some other form of quick fix, you can use the forceful self-dialogue format, suitably modified to apply to your own particular circumstances. In the following excerpt, the problem is alcohol abuse:

Irrational voice: 'I think I'll just pop out for a quick drink. One or two won't do me any harm.'

Rational voice: 'Yeah, I've heard that one before. Since when have you ever been known to stop at just one or two?'

Irrational voice: 'Ah, but that wasn't my fault, really. I just happened to bump into Derek and he insisted, really insisted on buying me a round.'

Rational voice: 'Oh sure! It's always somebody else's fault. What do they do – these so-called friends – twist your arm until it hurts and practically force you to drink?'

Irrational voice: 'Of course not! They're really nice guys.'

Rational voice: 'Nice guys my foot! That Derek's been dried out more times than the old raincoat he's had on his back for the last 20 years. It seems like attracts like!'

Irrational voice: 'Aw, c'mon. I'm not doing so bad now. Just a couple of drinks, that's all I ask. You know I can handle it.'

Rational voice (with sarcasm): 'Of course you can! After all it wasn't you who went out for "just a couple of drinks", and came home practically paralytic. Was it?'

Irrational voice: 'Well, OK, I guess I did get carried away on that occasion.'

Rational voice: 'Yes, and the next time you're going to get carried away, full stop. You even had to be restrained from getting into somebody else's car and driving it away, because you thought it was your own!'

Irrational voice: 'OK, but no great harm was done, was there? I survived, see.'

Rational voice: 'Rubbish! You've been stoned more times than you've had hot dinners. Just how do you know what you're doing when you're drunk? You got away with it last time, and maybe the next time, but what about the time after that, and the next, and the next? Sooner or later you're going to do yourself in. Your health's already going down the drain; your blood pressure is too high, your heart shows signs of trouble ahead and you talk about surviving! In the state you habitually are in these days, you could kill yourself, or worse still, somebody else!'

Irrational voice: 'Well, I don't know; maybe you're right.'

Rational voice: 'Maybe? You *know* I'm right! No more drinking from now on! And no nonsense about it, do you hear? None! That's it, full stop.'

It is important that the dialogue continues in this vein until the Rational Voice *convinces* the Irrational Voice.

Behaviour methods of change

It is a sad fact of human behaviour that once people become the victims of their own irrational thoughts and self-defeating feelings for any length of time, they tend to continue their neurotic behaviour even when they know it's foolish and they very much want to change it.

We tend to be habit-forming creatures. That has its good side because we can learn and acquire good habits, such as looking after our physical health. But we can just as easily acquire bad habits, such as over-eating, procrastinating, and enraging ourselves when our wishes are frustrated or blocked. Unfortunately, insight into these bad habits, and even a strong resolution to get rid of them isn't quite enough in most instances to make them disappear. Even worse, unless some action is taken to eliminate them, these habits often become worse.

Because of this, we can use a variety of behavioural methods to supplement our cognitive and emotive techniques. These techniques can be used in dealing with emotional problems and to help you to acquire a saner philosophy of living.

The use of homework assignments This is one such method. It is based on the principle that we all learn by doing. You can overcome many of your long-term anxieties by doing what it is you are most afraid of doing – and doing it, not just once or twice, but many times, and doing it 'cold turkey'.

Suppose you have been avoiding going for job interviews because you feel terribly nervous about doing so. You very much want to get a job, but the thought of being interviewed fills you with such acute anxiety that you deliberately avoid job interview opportunities because of the discomfort anxiety you experience. Thus you have a choice: either you force yourself to go for job interviews, brave the discomfort, and overcome your extreme fear, or else suffer with the fear for the rest of your life. In practice, you force yourself into doing whatever it is that you are irrationally afraid of, or are avoiding. At the same time, you use your 'anti-awfulizing' techniques to convince yourself that nothing truly dangerous will happen to you.

If you practise experiencing discomfort many times, you will show yourself that you can stand it. So, deliberately seek out some kind of discomfort, feel the discomfort and stay in the situation to convince yourself that doing what is uncomfortable is going to help you achieve your long-term goals. Negotiate homework assignments with yourself along these lines:

- Do things uncomfortably – things that are worth doing, that is — rather than wait until you feel comfortable before doing them.
- Do things *un*confidently rather than wait until you feel confident. You gain confidence by doing.
- Do things without being certain of the outcome. You don't have to be certain. Again, you learn by doing.

Your purpose in carrying out these assignments is not just to solve a discomfort problem, but also to encourage you to develop a long-range hedonistic philosophy. As you practise staying in an uncomfortable situation and at the same time practise convincing yourself that it is only unpleasant and inconvenient, you will overcome your extreme fear and your low frustration tolerance and see that you can stand the supposedly unbearable discomfort.

But a word of warning! Adopt an assignment which you find challenging, but not overwhelming. While we don't want you to tackle things that are easy and comfortable for you, neither do we want you to become discouraged as a result of failing to do something that is at present overwhelming for you. Our advice, therefore, is seek out challenges but not overwhelming experiences. As you succeed in doing that, you can take on bigger and bigger challenges. But don't, unless there are good reasons for it, throw yourself in at the deep end. And don't opt for the easy, unchallenging solution.

Overcoming obstacles to change

We've already drawn your attention to the need for persistence in working to overcome your discomfort problems. Unfortunately, some people don't persist long enough; they give up too soon. What is it that stops these people from putting into practice the advice they get to work and practise vigorously, often and persistently? They know that that is what they need to do if they are going to throw off the shackles they've picked up over the years and which are still impeding them from leading a more satisfying existence. They know what to do, all right. But they don't do it! Why not? There are three reasons for this and we will illustrate these with some typical responses from people who begin the process of working through their problems and who have willingly accepted their activity homework assignments, but who fail to do them systematically – or even fail to do them at all.

Cognitive-emotive dissonance

Don't be put off by that heavy-sounding technical term. You could translate it as 'The Neurotic Fear of Feeling a Phoney'. It can be explained quite simply as follows.

As you work towards change and begin to feel you are making some change, you feel 'unnatural' as you gradually strengthen your rational beliefs. You believe that you must feel natural at all times. You tend to think: 'This isn't me, I won't be me!' What is happening is that you fear you will lose your identity if you relinquish your irrational beliefs. It's like losing a part of you which you've had a long time and have got used to. Dr MC Maultsby Jr, explains it this way:

> 'The only phoney human beings existing in the real world outside our heads are mannequins. You are alive; therefore you cannot be either a mannequin or a phoney human being. Also, it is impossible not to be yourself. If you are not yourself, then who can you be? So, if fear of being a phoney is your only problem, you can solve it very easily by merely being unwilling to be afraid of events which can't possibly occur.'

Another way to look at this fear of feeling a phoney is to use the analogy of undertaking a physical exercise regimen. Let's suppose you have been out of condition for some time. Your muscles have become flabby, you easily get out of breath and many simple activities are an effort. When you start on an exercise programme to tone-up your muscles, improve your circulation and reduce your resting pulse rate, you will feel strange at first as you do the exercises. 'This isn't me!' you'll tell yourself. But as you persist and proceed to improve your physique, and your general health improves, you will feel quite at home with your exercise regime. The longer you maintain it, the better you will feel until a point arrives when you will actually miss doing your exercises should some circumstance momentarily interrupt your daily schedule!

Think of your homework assignments as a way of developing *emotional* muscle. You may feel strange and uncomfortable at first, but that feeling will pass if you persist at it. *Persistence is the key*. Print those words on a 5 × 3 card and carry it about with you in your wallet or handbag. Read the card several times daily to remind yourself of the value of sticking to your programme for change.

To summarize, new things will often feel strange or unnatural at first. That's quite common and quite natural. If you feel you are 'not being you', keep doing your assignments while you're feeling strange or 'phoney', stay in the uncomfortable situation until you do feel comfortable doing it, or at least less uncomfortable. As you do that, convince yourself that you don't have to feel you are you. If you persist, quite soon you will get over the feeling of strangeness and your new rational attitude will become part of you.

'I'll become a robot!'

This fear of becoming an unfeeling robot is expressed by people who believe that living rationally means becoming devoid of all feeling, rather than experiencing appropriate negative emotions, such as sadness, regret, etc. These people simply misunderstand the goals of rationality. Far from playing down human feelings, we take the view that the expression of feeling is a basic human attribute. We espouse the goal of joyful living while not denying the legitimate place of appropriate negative feelings such as sadness, regret, sorrow and disappointment. What we do try to minimize are *inappropriate* feelings such as anxiety despair, hostility and self-denigration. These self-destructive emotions and behaviours do nothing to promote human happiness.

Low frustration tolerance

Yes, it's your old 'friend' LFT again. This is probably the commonest reason why people balk at doing their activity homework assignments. 'Well, what did you tell yourself just before you decided not to carry out your assignment?' we might ask. Then we are told: 'I just said to myself, I'll do it later'. When we pursue the issue and ask: 'But why didn't you do it right there and then when you first thought of it?' a typical answer is: 'Well, it's too hard! It shouldn't be so hard! I should be able to get better without doing that kind of work!'

It's a kind of Catch-22 situation, isn't it? First, you are trying to overcome a discomfort problem. Then you discover that in order to do that you have to do something which is itself uncomfortable. Tough! If we knew of an easier way we'd tell you about it. But the fact is that there is no easy way. As we tell our clients: 'You have a choice: either you work and practise doing uncomfortable things until you overcome your problem – which you definitely can do in a relatively short time while accepting a time-limited degree of discomfort; or, you can stay as you are and remain in the Comfort Trap forever with all that that means in terms of your overall level of satisfaction with life. So, what is it to be? The choice is yours.'

Don't allow yourself to be discouraged. As a first step in getting you going, actively and vigorously dispute these irrational beliefs: 'It's too hard!; it shouldn't be so hard; I should be able to get better without doing that kind of work.'

Once you convince yourself that these iBs make no sense and you give them up, you will have a much easier time doing your homework assignments, especially if you convince yourself of the rational alternative beliefs. Thus, you will truly realize: 'Sure, it's hard and there's no reason why it shouldn't be hard. If it's hard, it's hard. If I should be able to get better without hard work, then I would. Obviously, no such "should" exists. So I'd better realistically buckle down to doing my assignments, and tolerate the discomfort in order to realize my long-term objectives.'

Use self-management principles

If you still experience difficulty in doing your activity homework assignments or in persisting with them, you can resort to self-management principles to help you overcome your LFT. Select something you enjoy doing, such as reading, listening to music, cooking, knitting, drawing or painting, or having a meal with friends, and make the performance of that enjoyable activity contingent upon doing the homework activity you have set yourself. That might be going for a job interview or writing a report or doing something important that needs to be done promptly but which you've been putting off. If you fail to do your assignment, no performance of the enjoyable activity!

If that doesn't work, try penalizing yourself. Contract with yourself to carry out some boring task, or something you abhor doing, such as cleaning the bathroom, if you fail to carry out your homework activity.

An effective penalty is to deposit with a friend a sum of money you can scarcely afford to lose. You then instruct your friend to donate that money to a cause you particularly detest if you fail to carry out your assignment. The use of immediate rewards for doing difficult or uncomfortable assignments as well as the employment of strict, quickly enforced penalties immediately following a failure to carry out an assignment, can be very effective in persuading you to carry out your assignments in short order.

Dealing with relapse

Locating vulnerability factors

It sometimes happens that after having made reasonable progress, people do fall back. If this happens, refuse to blame yourself for falling back. Blaming won't do you any good and will probably interfere with your ability to deal constructively with the matter. Look for your 'vulnerability factors' (VFs). An example will make clear what we mean. Let's suppose that you are trying to overcome a problem of shopaholicism. Some of your VFs might be as follows:

1. Having a period may be a time when you are feeling particularly uncomfortable. When that happens, it's maybe not a very good idea to go shopping down the high street as you may be tempted then to indulge your self by compulsively purchasing 'comfort' items rather than necessary items.
2. You may recognize that you are vulnerable when you are with friends who really encourage you to buy things impulsively. In that case you can avoid their company until you feel less vulnerable.

Similarly, if you have a compulsive eating problem, you can restructure your environment in such a way that you reduce your temptations to eat. For example, when shopping, take just enough money to cover the cost of essential grocery items and avoid the purchase of foods which you find tempting and which would cause you problems.

You may find it useful to make a list of your vulnerability factors so that you are aware of those times when you are likely to be under more pressure to give in to a quick fix. Typical VFs are:

1. Rejection following a date or job interview.
2. Feeling low during your period or because of PMT.
3. Feeling uptight after a particularly tough, stressful day at home or in the office.
4. Workaholicism: when things are not going well in some part of your

life, you may be vulnerable to compulsively absorbing yourself in an excessive amount of work.

5. Chocaholicism: when you feel an urge to binge on chocolate, avoid going near shops which sell chocolate or foods containing chocolate, such as chocolate gateaux. Steer clear of confectionery counters in supermarkets. Try to satisfy your craving for something sweet by eating fresh fruit, or drinking pure fruit juices.

6. Gambling: feeling an urge to gamble can get you into trouble once you start. You can help yourself by avoiding places where race meetings are scheduled and giving betting shops a wide berth. Find someone, or a group of people who enjoy playing competitive board-type games such as chess or draughts and join them. However, avoid such games if betting on the outcome is involved.

In all cases you can stay away from friends or situations which may trigger your vulnerability factors. If you can't stay away, or wish to strengthen your new philosophy, then you have to face up to the situations and practise your new philosophy. You will have to go over it strongly and vigorously. Doing it in a weak namby-pamby manner will not help you much!

Use imagery

Another way of dealing with relapse is to use imagery. In your mind's eye imagine seeing yourself facing temptations and practise seeing yourself thinking rationally in facing these temptations and not giving in to the addiction. The idea of using imagery positively is, of course, to help strengthen your rational philosophy.

Self-help books: why they don't work

What happens when people buy self-help books? Well, for a start, people expect that the knowledge in these books will go into them passively, and that that passive knowledge will make them change. In other words, reading will do the trick without anything else. Or, even reading plus a little action will be enough to send them on their way to happiness. People believe that once they've understood something, *and* that they've put it into practice, maybe one or two times, and have been successful, that they don't have to do any more work. So they may get discouraged when change doesn't magically come about through 1. just reading it passively; and 2. reading it plus acting on the advice on one or two occasions. The idea that change is easy is a beguiling thought – especially to people who have some degree of LFT, which just about includes everybody!

The fact of the matter is that you can use self-help books *if* you are truly committed to really putting their ideas into practice, and keep *practising* and *practising* them. But that is precisely one of the things which people who believe they need to be comfortable, feel quite uncomfortable about: practising! They hate the idea of having to do work and make themselves uncomfortable now in order to benefit later. Thus, they even bring their discomfort disturbance to self-help books!

The message of most good self-help books is: we can give you good information and good suggestions for putting it into practice. But *you* need to do the practice, and you need to *keep doing* the practice; and that's uncomfortable. So our advice is, get over your dire need for comfort about reading self-help books and using self-help books.

Finally, although we have focused in this book on discomfort problems that people have mainly as a consequence of LFT, we would remind you that people also have uncomfortable feelings due to their ego problems and they make themselves disturbed about the discomfort of the emotional consequences of these ego problems. As a companion to this book we thoroughly recommend Paul Hauck's book, *Hold Your Head Up High* (Sheldon, 1991) and, as we suggested in Chapter 5, use Paul's excellent book to help you deal with your ego problems.

One final message: realize that tolerating discomfort in order to aid goal attainment and long-range happiness is the healthy and rational alternative to demands for immediate gratification. Acting on this realization, repeatedly, is what counts. We wish you every success!

Index